Hybrid Learning

Hybrid Learning

The Perils and Promise of Blending Online and Face-to-Face Instruction in Higher Education

JASON ALLEN SNART

 PRAEGER

AN IMPRINT OF ABC-CLIO, LLC
Santa Barbara, California • Denver, Colorado • Oxford, England

Library of Congress Cataloging-in-Publication Data

Snart, Jason Allen, 1973–
    Hybrid learning : the perils and promise of blending online and face-to-face instruction in higher education / Jason Allen Snart.
        p. cm.
    Includes bibliographical references and index.
    ISBN 978-0-313-38157-7 (hard copy : alk. paper) — ISBN 978-0-313-38158-4 (ebook)
    1. Blended learning.   2. Distance education—Computer-assisted instruction.
3. Education—Effect of technological innovations on.   4. Educational technology—Computer-assisted instruction.   I. Title.
    LB2395.7.S55   2010
    371.3—dc22   2010002197

ISBN: 978-0-313-38157-7
EISBN: 978-0-313-38158-4

14 13 12 11 10   1 2 3 4 5

This book is also available on the World Wide Web as an eBook.
Visit www.abc-clio.com for details.

Praeger
An Imprint of ABC-CLIO, LLC

ABC-CLIO, LLC
130 Cremona Drive, P.O. Box 1911
Santa Barbara, California 93116-1911

This book is printed on acid-free paper ∞

Manufactured in the United States of America

This book is dedicated to my family, above all to my wife, Alison, and to our daughter, Jenna Arlen Snart, whose birth, on December 30, 2008, punctuated my research and writing with a profound exclamation point!

Pedagogically, education by correspondence is almost terra incognita.

—John Noffsinger, *Correspondence Schools* (1926)

Contents

Acknowledgments

This book would not have been possible without the time and effort provided by so many people who talked with me, often at great length, about their experiences developing, teaching, and managing hybrid courses and programs. Of particular note are my colleagues at the College of DuPage who have been so generous with their time and open about their experiences: Ada Wainwright, Naheed Hasan, Lois Stanciak, and Mitch Fisher. Others at the college who shared their knowledge and insight include Nancy Conradt, Denise Cote, and Christine Kickels. And, for all those numbers, thanks to Prudy Widlak in the Office of Research and Planning.

Special thanks also go to Natasja Larson, the Master of Education in Educational Studies Program Administrator at the University of Alberta, and to Emily Conradt, whose perspective as a graduate student provided so many important insights about what it is like to learn in a hybrid program. I am grateful to many others for generously sharing their expertise, their experience, and their insight: Kathie Gossett, Old Dominion University; Bret Ingerman, Vassar College; Alan Wilson, York College-City University of New York Writing Program; Amy Beasley, Lane Community College; Beth Hewett, Professional Development Consultant with the National Council of Teachers of English; Bob Whipple, Jr., Creighton University; Bradley Dilger, Western Illinois University (go Gators!); Monica Hahn, Community College of Philadelphia; Deanna Mascle, Morehead State University; Randy Garrison,

University of Calgary; Ed Nagelhout, University of Nevada; Eileen Connell, W. W. Norton and Company; Marty Bolger, now a graduate of Elmhurst College; Patricia Donahue, Lafayette College; Rick Branscomb, Salem State College; Russ Hunt, St. Thomas University; Lori A. Russell-Chapin, Bradley University; Sonja L. Andrus, Collin College; and Scott Warnock, Drexel University, whose interesting blog, "Online Writing Teacher," can be found at http://onlinewritingteacher.blogspot.com.

Special thanks to my colleagues in the College of DuPage English department, Linda Elaine and Jackie McGrath, who worked through early drafts of this manuscript with keen eyes. Robert Hutchinson, my editor at Praeger, provided invaluable help in shepherding the book into its final state.

Introduction

In his 1926 book on the then-burgeoning business of correspondence schools, John Noffsinger relegated their educational status to terra incognita. The processes and outcomes associated with teaching and learning by correspondence could not be adequately monitored, measured, regulated, or evaluated relative to traditional, classroom learning. Distance education by correspondence, all the vogue in Noffsinger's day, would eventually become what we know today as online learning.

A variation on the idea of learning at a distance is now emerging across the higher education landscape. It brings together elements of the traditional classroom environment and elements of modern online delivery. Hybrid, or blended, learning represents for many a potential best-of-both-worlds educational model, one that might draw on the most effective aspects of face-to-face (f2f) and online instruction. But, like the correspondence education of yesteryear, hybrid learning risks becoming terra incognita in the landscape of higher education without informed decision making early on.

Many economic, technological, and demographic factors are converging today to encourage institutional efforts—sometimes aggressive efforts—to develop blended learning options for students as quickly and as broadly as possible. The promise of blending face-to-face and online instruction in a delivery mode that will grow enrollments and fatten coffers, all while alleviating problems of limited classroom space and overstretched campus resources, may seem just too good to pass up for some schools. But thoughtless urgency and uninformed decision making will push hybrid learning into perilously uncharted territory, where it will be susceptible to the worst fates of online and correspondence education—just another element of managed education adhering more to the logic of business than to the common sense of sound pedagogy.

The hazards in the future of hybrid learning are especially worrisome if all of the constituencies with a stake in effective teaching and learning—faculty, administrators, support staff, parents, and students—are not prepared for informed discussion and action. What do we need to know, do, and discuss in order to ensure that hybrid learning develops into the successful educational model that so many involved in higher education are persuaded it can be?

This book explores hybrid teaching and learning in the broad cultural and historical terms we need to understand if we are to avoid its becoming a new terra incognita. But this book is equally concerned with the specifics of how blended teaching and learning are actually taking place. What do hybrid classes look like, and are there any similarities among them? Must they be high-tech, or low-tech, to produce successful learning results? What has motivated students to take hybrid classes and faculty to design and teach them? And what effect does the institutional rhetoric that surrounds hybrids have on the daily activities of those taking and teaching the courses?

Beyond classroom specifics, we need to see hybrid teaching and learning against a number of other broad backgrounds. What is the history of this delivery mode? Does blended learning have educational precedent in learning modes other than strictly online delivery?

And how is technology being used—and why is it being used—by so many people today outside the classroom? What implications do popular Web and Internet-based applications have for blended learning in higher education?

Finally, what assumptions and beliefs prevail among educators, administrators, and students about hybrid teaching and learning? Are these assumptions well-founded, or might they be leading us into parts unknown and treacherous?

METHOD

This book is meant to be descriptive and suggestive, rather than prescriptive. It does not aim to tell teaching professionals what they must do to ensure success in specific college classes. Teaching faculty ought to be the final arbiters when it comes to individual syllabus design and pedagogy, though such individual choices are inevitably most productive when they arise from ongoing dialogue with colleagues.

Blended or hybrid learning presents an opportunity for faculty to re-imagine and retool their curricular design and teaching strategies. Blended classes do not necessarily require anything high-tech, but the opportunity to incorporate interesting and exciting digital technologies into courses should be given careful consideration.

Ultimately, individual faculty will make decisions about how to construct their hybrid classes and what digital tool(s) they will want to learn about and use. But making blended learning effective—allowing it to live up to its potential—will also take institutional vision. The responsibility for achieving educational success, however that might be defined, through blended learning should not be laid at the feet of any single constituency within higher education. It must be shared by faculty, administration, and student support personnel alike.

The "At a Glance" profiles provided in the appendix to this work outline core concerns that all stakeholders should be aware of when it comes to blended learning as an institutional prerogative. However, these profiles, like the rest of the book itself, are offered as suggestively forward-looking, not statically prescriptive. We look at how hybrid courses are currently being designed and taught both within a single institution and across a number of different schools. We evaluate some promising possibilities for applying online applications to hybrid course design and delivery with a view to improving the overall learning experience—both for the educator and for the student. We focus on the crucial question of how hybrid courses can be most thoughtfully and effectively designed to meet 21st-century learning goals in the context of emerging workplace realities, which stress to a greater and greater degree collaborative content creation and communal knowledge building and sharing.

Although the hybrid model is gaining wider visibility in higher education specifically as a combination of online and face-to-face learning, blended teaching in its broadest sense is not by any means new. For years, individual teachers have been combining face-to-face classroom activities with out-of-class learning of various kinds. This has often been happening with no broader institutional context, or support, in place. For example, institutional mechanisms may not be in place to alert students before arriving to class on the first day that they have signed up for a hybrid class. IT support or guidance specific to blended learning may not be in place. Organized faculty development opportunities may be limited or nonexistent. And there may be little in the way of contractually agreed upon or institutionally negotiated policies for such basic matters as how office hours must be accounted for when a faculty member's teaching load includes hybrid courses. Yet many individual faculty members have, for years, been successfully reconfiguring class time by combining face-to-face with online or out-of-class learning.

And this reminds us that hybrid learning derives from a varied set of ancestors; it is not just a new twist on online learning. Equally a progenitor of the hybrid model is the long tradition in higher education of field and experiential studies. In an English composition class that is offered as part of an experiential program, for example, students might meet as a group for a few face-to-face classroom sessions. The rest of the class time occurs face-to-face, but not in the traditional classroom space. A field and experiential class might travel as a group to a particular destination, treating the world as a classroom. Basic course goals are folded into what can often be intensive learning experiences. Beyond meeting basic course objectives, students grow emotionally as they bond with their instructor and with classmates, and they mature through the self-knowledge that often comes with experiential learning of this kind. The hybrid model, understood in this broad sense, can provide a much richer learning experience than can traditional classroom instruction alone.

Even as we consider technology-based blended learning more specifically, experiential courses that blend two very different learning modes can provide a more useful precedent than does the history of strictly online course delivery taken alone. The field and experiential model allows us to understand how learning objectives can be met, and often surpassed, in many different learning environments, ones not necessarily as structured or controlled as the traditional classroom. Understanding hybrid or blended teaching models that employ face-to-face and online components as having long and varied institutional precedents may also help to convince resistant or skeptical faculty, parents, students, or administrators that blended learning is—or at least can be—a viable educational model. Nor is blended learning, even as a member of the larger e-learning family, necessarily going to be predisposed to the same problems that have plagued strictly online learning.

But while individual faculty have been trading classroom learning time for other learning experiences for many years, and while such blended models as field and experiential studies have, in many cases, a long institutional history, we are right now, as we move out of the first decade of the 21st century, seeing the nascent period of organized, institution-wide growth in hybrid learning that involves traditional classroom and online learning modes. In other words, many college and universities are—as institutions—either going or are about to go hybrid. Blended learning is more and more becoming one of the standard delivery options available to students.

In fact, where we stand now with blended learning looks much like the pre-boom period we saw in the early 1990s for strictly online learning. Writing in 1989, in his foreword to Kamala Anandam's collection, *Transforming Teaching with Technology*, Ken King, then president of Educom, observed that "information technology is starting to change higher education in major ways."[1] Scarcely a decade later, Sir John Daniel, former vice chancellor of The Open University, the distance learning university founded and funded by the British government, wrote that "the dot-com frenzy of late 1999 and early 2000 was a nerve-wracking time."[2]

The fundamental paradigm shift away from traditional classroom instruction and toward online learning that happened in the 1990s—a shift whose effects reverberate today—was one of the most ground-shaking that higher education has ever experienced. It was a game changer, and hybrid and blended learning may be ready to change the game again.

In the case of online learning in the past, numerous individual faculty, the so-called early adopters, were using various online tools to manage and teach classes. However, from these scattered instances, online learning became a highly visible institutional priority on campuses across the United States. Entire online programs were developed, as were the institutional services required to maintain and administer booming online course development and enrollment. It is a truism now that online learning has become a permanent fixture of higher education, no more unusual or alternative a delivery mode than traditional face-to-face learning.

Blended learning is not there yet. Some in the teaching profession have even experienced changes in local departmental or institutional leadership that result in a move away from blended learning rather than toward it.[3] In other words, depending on whom you ask and when, blended learning might not necessarily be here to stay, much less might it be the next high-demand learning model for the 21st century.

But we are definitely at a point when blended learning is going to become a widely visible hot-button issue, on the institutional level, at many campuses. So now is the time to consider blended learning in broad historical and cultural terms, time to examine how the hybrid model is currently being deployed, and time to imagine what hybrids might look like, and what they might enable, with some creative and informed decision making.

TERMINOLOGY

The reader will notice that the terms "hybrid" and "blended" have been used to this point more or less interchangeably. Other terms that describe the same basic curricular model include "mixed mode" and sometimes just the catchall "flexible," though this term is particularly misleading. But what better evidence that the field of hybrid/blended learning is in its nascent stages than this still-shifting terminology?

Books on the subject often employ the term "blended," as in the collection edited by Anthony G. Picciano and Charles D. Dziuban, *Blended Learning: Research Perspectives.*[4] Many people prefer the term "blended" because it has a less mechanized or scientific feel than does the term "hybrid." In popular culture, the concept of the hybrid can sometimes connote the negative sense of identity-erasing assimilation, though we are finding the opposite to be true more and more of the time. One notable example of the implicit dark side of hybridity is the Borg race from the *Star Trek: The Next Generation* and *Voyager* series. The Borg, from "cyborg," an organic/synthetic hybrid, operate as a collective mind, assimilating all that they encounter. The phrase "resistance is futile" gained pop culture currency thanks to the Borg's appearance in the *Star Trek: The Next Generation* episode "The Best of Both Worlds."[5] Interestingly, this best-of-both-worlds idea, and often the exact phrase, is sometimes applied to hybrid learning. The University of Massachusetts's "UMass Online" homepage provides a typical example: "Blended Learning: Combining the Best of Both Worlds." Or see the homepage for Sandhills Community College's Evening Hybrid Program: "The Evening Hybrid Program provides the best of both worlds."[6]

The Borg are never referred to explicitly as hybrid, however. This is an important rhetorical point because we note that, while a basic idea can be in place (the best of both worlds, for example), it is ultimately the precise language that circulates around the idea, brings it into being, that communicates its cultural value, be it positive (the hybrid car), negative (the Borg), or neutral.[7] Perhaps the key distinction is between the idea of combination as assimilation—the erasure of distinctive characteristics in favor of a homogeneous singularity—and that of combination as hybridizing. This latter sense, as we will explore later on, more often connotes the creation of something new but without destroying the defining characteristics of the original ingredients...a rhetorically and culturally value-positive version of the best-of-both-worlds premise.

The rhetoric of hybridity has, in fact, gained considerable cultural currency. You find it in the most surprising places. I picked up a shoe box in a retail store one day because printed across the top, in bold lettering, was the phrase "100% Hybrid." An odd contradiction, connoting both purity and multiplicity, but this phrase captures exactly the kind of positive implications that the term "hybrid" carries. The shoe brand was Keen, whose latest advertising campaign promotes "the Hybrid Life." Indeed, visit the Keen Web site and you can join the "HybridLife Community" or learn about Keen's "Hybrid.Care" nonprofit programs. Of course, you can also "Buy Now."[8]

Popular and consumer culture associations relative to the term "hybrid" aside, however, the term "blended" may eventually gain popular academic traction simply because the Library of Congress uses "blended learning" as a major subject heading. So a library catalogue subject search for "blended learning" will return available results. A subject search for "hybrid learning" redirects researchers to "blended learning." This implicitly privileges "blended learning" over "hybrid learning" (though both searches can return useful results). A subject search for "hybrid" alone is likely to return a rather extensive list of subheadings, from "hybrid corn" to "hybrid vehicles."

This latter phenomenon draws me to the term "hybrid": it denotes a category with wide cultural application, especially now, in the age of hybrid cars...and corn. That the term "hybrid" can sometimes imply dark motives of assimilation and the erasure of difference makes it that much more interesting, retaining as it does a sense of semantic nuance and discursive subtlety. The idea of the hybrid—and thus of hybrid learning—seems less a model with roots solely in the world of higher education and more a cultural dynamic with implications for and applications to a number of different fields.

The group of educators that constitute the "Best Practices for Online Writing Instruction," which is a part of the Conference on College Composition and Communication (CCCC) organization, has tried to delineate a distinction between hybrid and blended learning. Beth Hewett, the CCCC "Best Practices for Online Writing Instruction" committee chair, has explained that "'blended' means meeting most of all classes in a computer lab/classroom and working both via networked computers and face-to-face"; "'hybrid' means meeting classes both in a traditional classroom and in a computer lab/classroom (often done in a one day on/one day off arrangement)."[9] Hewett further clarified this distinction when we corresponded, noting that, in the committee's vision, the blended learning model "seems to us to be one where both face-to-face interaction and computer-mediated interaction is always available at one time."[10] In this sense, blended learning still means that most class meetings take place face-to-face. Hybrid learning, on the other hand, may involve a substantial non-face-to-face online learning component.

It may be less useful to arrive at consensus on one term just yet or to argue for the rightness of one label over another than it is to explore the very unsettledness of the terminology itself. For every book that employs "blended," we could likely find an article that uses "hybrid." Take Margie Martyn's "The Hybrid Online Model"[11] or Catherine Gouge's "Hybrid Courses and the Future of Writing Programs"[12] as just two examples. The Sloan Consortium, publisher of *Blended Learning: Research Perspectives*, asks visitors to its Web site, "What term does your institution use?" Options include "Blended," "Hybrid," "Mixed Mode," and "Other." Of the more than 1,000 votes recorded, 51 percent indicate that "Blended" is the preferred term; 39 percent indicate that "Hybrid" is preferred; 4 percent indicate "Mixed Mode"; and 6 percent (more than those who selected "Mixed Mode") indicate "Other."[13]

The terms "blended," "hybrid," "mixed mode," and even "flexible" are used more or less interchangeably throughout this book, except where it makes sense to delineate clear distinctions. The choice to let the terminology shift is meant to reflect the nascent state, not of indecision but of predecision, that we are seeing as higher education thinks broadly about mixed-mode learning that combines face-to-face and online instruction.

So, to summarize, the larger method of the book is to combine description with forward-looking vision and to offer recommendations rather than prescriptions, for we find ourselves at a point when informed decision making and informed debate about blended learning need to be happening if they are not already, at the institutional level, across the higher education landscape.

With the potential to affect the very face of education as has online learning, hybrid learning should be of interest to stakeholders beyond just the classroom: clearly, new modes of teaching will affect educators and students, but equally affected will be administrators, student support personnel, and parents and family members of college and university students. In fact, when it comes to basic issues of education, we all have a stake in effective teaching and learning.

CHAPTER 1

The Resistant Early Adopter

We are living in an evermore media-rich—some would say media-saturated—environment. The subtitle of Todd Gitlin's 2001 book, *Media Unlimited,* makes the point precisely: "How the Torrent of Images and Sounds Overwhelms Our Lives."[1] Enabling this media torrent is technology in all its various manifestations, from netbooks and smartphones to Internet-ready televisions and webcams. Of course, it is possible to ignore the torrent and to resist technology, especially as these can intrude on educational spaces. Indeed, educational spaces are sometimes conceived of as retreats from the media torrent of everyday life and the 24/7 immersion in technology that can be all too common for many people. The classroom often privileges the practices of reflection and deep analysis, neither of which finds a comfortable place in our sound-bite culture. Some thus argue that the more technology-dominated our everyday lives become, the less technology-dominated should be our educational spaces.[2]

The classroom in higher education has also traditionally privileged text-based learning. The typical college class is a biblio—or book—centric space. And perhaps resistance to change, as that change appears in the form of technology, should come as no surprise, given that the mandate laid upon college educators is to develop and refine basic competencies like reading, writing, and critical reasoning. These are, at least traditionally, text-based skills, and technology can often seem like little more than a distraction from these basic educational goals. For some, technology in education should ideally involve little more than computers as word processors if we are to maintain a literate society. But the notion of literacy is ever-expanding to include the ability to read, and create, visually rich Web pages, not just the pure text of the conventionally printed page.

In fact, technology in the form of the Web functions rather more effectively when it is deployed in ways that reconfigure the basic premises of linear, textual argument. That is, the Web communicates best, or it educates and engages most effectively, not when it is used to present a single thesis and to support that thesis in a linear fashion, as might the traditional college essay. The Web works best when it is used to reflect associative, nonlinear thinking.

For those academic disciplines whose traditions are grounded in the communication of ideas, or theses, in print, the seeming disruption of that grounding by technology can be unsettling. Mark Bauerlein has argued that "no generation has experienced so many techno-enhancements and produced so little intellectual progress."[3] And Robert Reid, a teaching assistant in the United Kingdom, thinks that "schools and colleges are awash with uninspiring technologies of questionable value."[4] These sentiments reflect a basic skepticism when it comes to technology in education: technology, rather than enhancing the learning experience, is working counter to it, and it is becoming a costly distraction.

For many, technology provides a visually—and often aurally—rich environment, but one that is text poor. The average Web user these days will notice that most sites employ very little text and certainly no blocks of text longer than a few lines or a short paragraph. So a vision of technology as just the text-poor Web can easily provoke resistance, if not at least a sense of unease, in many educators whose own scholarly backgrounds, traditions, and allegiances are based in printed text and whose teaching objectives include cultivating in students basic critical reading and writing skills.

From here it is easy to see how and why many educators react with no small measure of skepticism when it comes to integrating technology into their curricula. The root is, in part, a narrow and fuzzy notion of just what technology is. For many, technology simply means the Web. Resistance can be reinforced by the sense that a movement toward technology is de facto a movement away from the very traditions we are trying to introduce to students. Simplistically speaking, you can build a Web page or you can read *Moby Dick*. But you cannot do both.

Perhaps most crucial for making technology in the classroom realizable and productive for the least tech-savvy educator, or the most tech-resistant, is to understand that technology, in whatever form, works best when we can see and represent to others exactly what problem it is helping us to overcome. In other words, what does technology allow us to do better? In this sense, technology can more obviously become an educational enhancement (an addition to something) rather than an alternative (a replacement for something).

Part of being able to answer this question involves rethinking the term "technology." Any particular technology is simply a means, a series of steps, or a material tool for completing a task. The hammer and the wheel are technologies in this sense. So technology, in and of itself, need not suggest complexity, though it often does for many people. Certainly the printing press and the Internet are (or were) complex technologies for their time, but they share in common with much simpler technologies the fundamental characteristic that they can be employed to overcome a specific problem. The printing press can be used to produce many identical copies of a piece of text, where otherwise manual labor would be required in the form of industrious scribes to produce those copies. The Internet, as it was first conceived and as it is still sometimes used today, overcomes the problem of communicating efficiently and effectively over long distances, often among many individuals. And so the hammer, a simple tool if ever there was one, seems fundamentally different from a computer. However, as technologies, the hammer and wheel are, like the printing press and the Internet, just tools for overcoming a particular problem. How much more approachable does technology become when it is understood specifically as a means to overcome an existing, identifiable, problem? One sometimes hears that technology is a solution in search of a problem. Undoubtedly, part of effective technology use in the classroom involves identifying exactly what problem, or problems, technology can help us to confront.

We might also ask: what technologies do we all already use in the classroom to overcome the basic challenges of communicating ideas to a group of people? I personally know of no college professor who does not, at least on occasion, use chalk and chalkboard or dry erase marker and whiteboard. Chalkboards and whiteboards are not mechanically intricate technologies. They are not electric. They do not feature moving parts. But they are still technologies in the sense that they allow for a professor to communicate, on the spot, with a classroom full of students. A student's notebook is a technology, too, the purpose of which is to overcome the problem of recording information and ideas communicated by the professor in order to make future study and reference possible. So let us imagine that a couple of students show up to class, not with notebooks but with notebook computers. Certainly the computer is a much more intricate machine, but no more or less a technology, necessarily, than coil-bound, lined paper. The notebook and the notebook computer are used in this instance to overcome the same problem. Technology is too often misunderstood as necessitating a rejection of what has come before, when this need not actually be the case at all.

The simplified example of the notebook and notebook computer as equivalent technologies, at least inasmuch as they can be used to complete the same basic task, ultimately allows us to understand technology as most effective when responding to clearly identified, existing problems or obstacles. Understanding technology in this way can help us to make the case for incorporating new technologies (or what are often just more complex versions of old technologies) in the classroom that much stronger. Thus, an early chapter in the current work delineates some of the challenges that many colleges and universities face. These are the problems that, in some cases, technology can be deployed to address, if not actually to overcome.

Communications technologies that use the Internet—like the Web or virtual environments—are also too often conceived of as primarily passive learning tools. Because the Web is most effective as a visually rich communicator, it is commonly (mis)understood as most akin to the television, that most passive of technologies. But the Web need be anything but a passively consumed medium. Indeed, it is experiencing its greatest developments in areas of user-created content, collaboration, and circulation. Web building is easier than ever, and utilities like weblogs and wikis are free and easy to use.

In later chapters, we will look at a number of Web-based tools that can be used to facilitate student collaboration. We will explore in greater depth how so much of what is happening on and to the Web is moving in the direction of collaboratively generated content. In fact, collaboration is fast becoming a core competency on par with reading and writing. Collaboration, specifically online collaboration, is a basic skill toward which educators across disciplines are striving and that is particularly prized in many job fields. The Association of American Colleges and Universities (AAC&U), among many other educational organizations, has articulated a vision for education in the 21st century through its Greater Expectations initiative. A crucial component of this vision is collaboration: the new academy, according to the AAC&U, "values collaborative work, particularly in diverse groups."[5] The college essay, in its conventional and traditional application, is not a particularly collaborative exercise. It is, as many of us know, often a solitary endeavor.

Despite my being an English professor who uses technology and who teaches in a variety of delivery modes, I have not by any means abandoned the traditional essay as an assessment tool. I am, though, interested in extending to students multiple opportunities for collaborative work that is enabled by technology. I am an avid user of new technology—including multi-user virtual environments, blogs, and wikis—both for my everyday research and work as a college professor and as a significant component in my classes, which include composition and literature courses. I would even consider myself an early adopter.

First and foremost, though, I am a skeptic. I am as resistant as the next person when it comes to new ways of doing things in my classes. As Van B. Weigel argues in *Deep Learning for a Digital Age*, "use of technology in higher education should enrich and extend the student's exploration of new territory."[6] It should not be a shiny new toy used for the purposes of distraction or sheer entertainment.

So mine may represent a fairly typical professional position, though one that reflects apparently opposing ends of a spectrum: I am a resistant early adopter. I will thus be arguing for the inclusion of new technologies in course design and implementation, as means to enable student collaboration and expression, but with a specific focus on exactly why these technologies are worth exploring, since they often do require the investment of considerable time on the part of the teaching professor and of money and resources on the part of the institution as a whole.

Perhaps the fundamental challenge faced by students, faculty, and administrators alike, as we think about technology and education specifically in terms of making hybrid learning as effective as it can be, is exactly how to navigate the seemingly diametric poles of technology enthusiast and technology skeptic. Each end of the spectrum has something valuable to teach us.

CHAPTER 2

Challenges Facing Higher Education

The challenges addressed here are among those facing higher education that might be affected, at least to some degree, by increasing interest in hybrid and blended learning. Of course, my own teaching and course design experiences also shape the discussion, deriving as they do primarily from my work as an English professor at the College of DuPage (COD), a large, suburban community college in Glen Ellyn, Illinois.[1] But discussion remains parochial only in those cases when internal communications or unpublished data from my home institution bring into sharp focus the kinds of challenges that are faced by any number of institutions of higher education. The formal and informal communication that circulates within a school is often deeply revealing of larger institutional challenges and the responses to those challenges. However, such communication is not always, if ever, publicly available. Nor does the official institutional communication that does become public always capture what is being articulated informally in meetings and in department hallways. Relying solely on the public rhetoric of vision statements, mission statements, and institutional goals often provides less than half the story when it comes to how institutions are calling for growth in the area of blended learning or how the challenges facing higher education are actually being met on the ground level.

Examples from two-year institutions, like COD, are also generally useful because problems of student preparedness and student success are often acute at community colleges, though such problems are by no means limited to two-year schools. Community colleges can also enroll a significant percentage of first-time postsecondary students (i.e., those students who are the first in their family to attend college). Community college students are also likely to have considerable out-of-class commitments: many work multiple jobs and have family obligations, which can include taking care of parents and being parents. Additionally, community college students do not necessarily live on, or even near, campus. Technology, broadly speaking, can have an impact on how these issues figure into the learning experience for many students.

Some of the challenges detailed here, however, are not necessarily linked to blended learning in the institutional rhetoric that surrounds them. In other words, increasing hybrid class offerings is not always identified explicitly as a solution to certain institutional challenges. Often, diversifying course delivery options (to include traditional face-to-face, fully online, and blended models) is part of a constellation of related strategies that gain visibility across a campus.

Of immediate concern, though, for educators and students alike, are the issues surrounding the significant rise in institutionally generated mandates for increased hybrid and blended offerings. A top-down mandate shows up as a challenge facing higher education, simply because it can produce exactly the terra incognita of teaching and learning that John Noffsinger discovered in 1926 in writing *Correspondence Schools*. The issue is not even so much that the mandate for more hybrid courses too often comes from top administration down to faculty, although the reverse might be preferable. At issue is the rhetoric surrounding these kinds of mandates and what it reveals about institutional motivations in the mixed-mode direction. Equally problematic can be the kinds of assumptions about how increasing blended offerings will provide benefit to the institution rather than to the individual student learner, especially when or if institutions actually do see considerable faculty buy-in to blended learning across the curriculum.

MANAGING ENROLLMENT

Faculty on many campuses these days are feeling the push from administrators to increase hybrid course offerings. Often, the official statement of this kind of priority comes from the highest level of administration. At COD, for example, the college president presented a list of institutional priorities to assembled faculty and administrators. Coming in at 20 on a list of 38 institutional priorities was "Develop a plan for increased FTE [full time equivalent] credit enrollment by expanding blended learning."[2] Note the explicitly declared motivation behind expanded hybrid offerings: increased enrollment.[3]

Stating the blended learning priority in this way, as an enrollment generator, sets up a number of potential issues. Of course, the tacit assumption seems to be that the delivery mode itself, perhaps because it is believed to be flexible, will attract new students. It seems more likely that with increased hybrid course offerings enrollment would not grow—it would shift—as students already taking traditional, classroom courses opt for the blended model instead. So the immediate question emerges: how is a delivery mode, in and of itself, going to generate new enrollment? Clearly, an institution will have to sell those aspects of the delivery mode that distinguish it from other delivery modes. A quick look at the advertising on college and university Web sites for hybrid courses and programs reveals that this is exactly what is happening. Homepages for blended programs are peppered with statements about the benefits of blended learning as a flexible (though still effective) learning mode. So is it up to teaching faculty to design hybrid classes that conform to the advertising and that will indeed grow enrollment?

Best-practices research about how blended learning can be effective identifies online activities that engage students in higher-order or critical thinking as most beneficial. This means that online work is, ideally, more than basic test taking. We know that effective online content delivery includes multimedia, which can mean more demanding hardware and Internet connection requirements. And we know that students benefit from the sense of community that develops from regular, and sometime synchronous, communication between student and professor and among students themselves. Such pedagogically effective strategies, however, often appear as barriers to growing enrollment since they put greater demands on students taking the classes and on the degree of technical proficiency they might need—or might perceive that they need—in order to be successful in a class. Worth emphasizing is the effect that perception can have on students' class choices. A particular college course need not be technically demanding in actuality. But if a student perceives that a hybrid class will involve technology in some complicated way or that it will require technical skill beyond what might be necessary for the traditionally delivered version of that same course, that student is likely to gravitate toward the traditional classroom model. Fuzzy notions about exactly what a hybrid class is only exacerbate this problem.

Consider, then, that another of the COD president's stated goals (29th on the list of 38) was explicitly to "Identify and, where possible, eliminate or commence elimination of any barrier to growing enrollment."[4] We arrive at this unfortunate question: could certain components of online or blended learning courses—those that may in fact be most pedagogically effective—actually be considered, institutionally, as barriers to enrollment? We know further from student surveys that the primary reason students seek alternative delivery options is flexibility. One COD survey indicates that when asked to complete the statement "The primary reason you took the course online is," almost 70 percent of respondents chose the following answer: "flexibility of the online course allows me to choose the time and place to participate in the course."[5] Certainly, the draw of hybrid classes reflects this desire for increased flexibility over the traditional classroom delivery model. But what happens when a synchronous chat activity is included as part of the non-face-to-face component of a blended course? Could this meet with institutional resistance in that it works against the flexibility that is perceived to be the primary selling point—the facet of the delivery mode that will likely grow enrollment—of the course structure? Might we even encounter a situation in which individual faculty lose control over how they teach a class as administrations pursue highly visible priorities like enrollment growth? Imagine that online learning, within the blended format or not, becomes, by administrative mandate, flexible learning. And who decides what the term "flexible" even means? This situation involves basic challenges to academic freedom and will thus be deeply contentious.

What we see, as is often the case when it comes to blended learning, is that prima facie assumptions about how blended learning might work and what it can do on an institutional level do not necessarily match the realities of how such classes look on an individual basis when they are pedagogically most effective.

But the pressure on faculty to begin teaching hybrids can follow directly, and quickly, from much broader institutional mandates. For example, soon after the COD president's address, in which he laid out mandates for increased blended offerings and reduced barriers to enrollment, COD Communications faculty received an e-mail from the subdivision Associate Dean asking for more blended courses. The institutional priority moved quickly from a college-wide mandate, to the province of lower administrators who were tasked with soliciting hybrid classes, and finally to the faculty who were expected to create and teach these classes.

Administrative requests for increased hybrid offerings are not necessarily troubling in and of themselves, though again one might like the impetus for new teaching or course delivery strategies to come from faculty rather than to faculty. At issue is the time frame in which requests for more hybrid courses might be expected to unfold. The progression from institutional vision to practical reality might, from an administrative point of view, be expected to happen in a matter of weeks, especially where the call for increased blended learning opportunities ranks as a high institutional priority. But increasing hybrid offerings in any significant number in just weeks would be quick turnaround indeed, especially for a general professoriate that is not already well versed in teaching with technology and in alternative delivery formats. So how do higher education administrations imagine things will play out on the level of actual course design and delivery in this kind of time frame? Do an adequately prepared professoriate and sound instructional design take a back seat to growing enrollment?

In fact, "enrollment management" is a highly visible catchphrase across higher education. Accompanying rhetoric usually identifies a process whereby an institution continually re-evaluates the alignment of its current enrollment numbers, its enrollment goals, and its resources and mission. Too often, however, enrollment management is implicitly about increasing enrollment. Many schools, despite putative desires to increase their numbers, would do just as well to maintain or even decrease enrollment and to serve the students they do have more effectively.

The institutional goals that have been asserted for the College of DuPage again provide an instructive, though by no means unique, example. Among the top institutional priorities for 2007–2008 was "Implement enrollment management." This included the following objective: "Achieve enrollment target."[6] There is no direct statement that this target necessarily means an increase in enrollment; however, such is clearly the subtext. In fact, the *Daily Herald* newspaper reported in November 2008 on the then newly selected COD college president: "[his] ability to boost community college enrollment and fatten the coffers made him the perfect choice to lead College of DuPage. That's the perspective from College of DuPage Board Chairman Micheal McKinnon."[7] Despite any other fuzzy rhetoric about managing enrollment, it is clear that what was attractive about the new college president, at least in the eyes of the chairman of the college's Board of Trustees, among many others, was specifically his ability to increase enrollment. Efforts to grow enrollment, however, are often rooted in mistaken equations of progress—or the catchall, excellence—with sheer size.[8]

Enrollment management at many institutions is a perennial issue. In some cases, it truly does have as much to do with diversifying a student body as with generating income through increased tuition. But the fact is that many schools are feeling serious budgetary pressure, often the result of national, state, and local funding cuts. Growing enrollment is an obvious means by which to make up budget shortfalls, so colleges are often faced with the unavoidable choice to increase enrollment numbers. Growth, as a solution to institutional problems, however, can create as many challenges as it resolves. For example, more students need more classroom space, more parking, more complex and robust IT and library infrastructure, increased support staff capacity, and more elaborate academic support systems, including precourse testing, advising, and counseling services.

Given all of these factors, we begin to see how blended and hybrid learning can become so institutionally attractive. Flexible learning seems to provide the ideal delivery mode for schools that are looking to grow: you can offer more classes, to more students, without stressing the physical campus resources it takes to offer traditional, fully face-to-face classes. Throw into the mix the attractive public rhetoric that is the advertising for hybrid courses and programs—"the best of both worlds," "a brand new way to attend college"—and it is no surprise when higher education trends toward blended learning.[9] Does the logic that is driving this trend hold up, though? We will see as we continue to look more specifically at some of the challenges facing higher education.

SCHEDULING AND CLASSROOM SPACE

Providing classroom space and managing the scheduling of that space are fundamental challenges facing many colleges today. Part of the problem is that enrollment is not necessarily distributed evenly across the day. This is especially true for schools whose student populations typically have commitments, like work and family, in addition to school. A student population with significant extracurricular responsibilities will be looking to finish classes for the day with enough hours left to work a full-time job and/or care for a child. Evenings, too, might represent a high-demand time, whereas afternoon classes that occupy a large portion of the middle of the day do not tend to draw many students. This uneven distribution can lead to cramped classrooms in the morning but ghost-town conditions come late afternoon.[10]

While issues of space are not limited to big schools, such issues can be more acute when raw enrollment numbers are high. Consider that the largest single-campus, two-year college in the United States, Mt. San Antonio College in Walnut, California, reports a credit headcount (a direct indicator of student numbers) of 29,079. Santa Monica College enrolls 28,337 students, and Palomar College enrolls 26,118.[11] Larger state schools often report enrollment in excess of 50,000.[12]

Increasingly, institutions may be attracted by the perceived benefits that derive from the turn to hybrid learning, especially when it comes to addressing basic resource-demand issues like classroom space.

Faculty are likely to argue that pedagogy should always drive educational innovation and curricular (re)design, but institutions will most certainly see the practical implications of blended learning on the brick-and-mortar conditions of their everyday operations.

In the late 1990s, the University of Central Florida (UCF) was so pressed for space that it rented classrooms in a local high school. UCF even rented space in a local movie theater, which was used as a classroom. Steven Sorg, assistant vice president for distributed learning at UCF, commented, "We didn't serve popcorn, but we used the seats and they served as lecture halls." Focused efforts to increase hybrid offerings at UCF, along with new campus construction, helped to alleviate the problem of limited physical classroom space. Sorg admitted that, prior to substantial increases in alternative delivery courses, "We were searching for space wherever we could find it."[13]

But let us unpack some of the assumptions that are associated with increased blended offerings relative to issues of space.

Imagine what happens when faculty take up the charge—the institutional priority—for increased hybrid offerings in significant numbers. The assumption, institutionally, may be that this will provide a boon to the management of classroom space. Underlying this broader assumption, though, are a number of basic premises. One is that a hybrid or blended class will divide time equally: 50 percent face-to-face and 50 percent online. Such a division of time may be an option for many faculty members, and it has its benefits in terms of a regularized and predictable schedule for students, but there is nothing to say that class time need be divided in this way. Some educators may prefer to reduce face-to-face time by only a few classes, here and there, within a semester. So classroom meetings may still constitute 70 percent or more of a course. And the remaining 30 percent online time may not occur on a regular basis.

Increasing blended course offerings primarily as a response to limited physical campus space, we realize, requires that the division of course time become an institutionally mandated 50/50 split. Otherwise, how would a single classroom serve two classes?

To extend this scenario yet further: imagine that an institution requires that all hybrids must split time 50/50. To effectively double classroom space, two teaching faculty members would have to be scheduled as a pair: one will teach a Tuesday/Thursday class at a particular time of day and meet face-to-face on Tuesday, while the other faculty member's class meets face-to-face on Thursday. Not only would someone other than the faculty members themselves decide how much time would be spent online and how much on face-to-face contact, but each faculty member would also be required to meet in the classroom on a predetermined day. Such intrusions into basic course design and teaching method are likely to meet with considerable resistance.

A slightly different scenario might involve a single faculty member, perhaps assigned two sections of the same course, with a view to having those two classes occupy the physical space of just one class. In other words, a faculty member might be required to create two different hybrid versions of a single class, one that schedules a face-to-face meeting early in the week and trades a later meeting in that week for online work, while another version of the same course reverses the f2f and online components, meeting in person later in the week and trading the earlier f2f class time for online work. Once again, faculty members are unlikely to begin tailoring curricula in this way, effectively doubling their course prep work, to meet institutional goals of maximizing classroom space.

Finally, though—and this now assumes that an institution could sell the idea of administratively managed hybrids to a large, cooperative group of faculty—imagine the scheduling puzzle that results when hundreds of teachers go hybrid, not just the two in our example. And, of course, not all classes will fall on Tuesday/Thursday. What about Monday/Wednesday/Friday classes, or once-a-week meetings, or classes that do not run the traditional 16-week semester—the complications abound. We see that the assumption that effective management of classroom space will be a benefit derived from increasing blended learning opportunities may be deeply mistaken. Scheduling itself may, in fact, become intractably complicated as more faculty teach in the hybrid mode. The chance that classroom space will be freed up by significantly increased hybrid offerings seems less and less likely.

Might as well serve popcorn in the movie theater lecture hall after all.

ALIGNING LEARNING OBJECTIVES

In addition to motivations for increasing hybrid course offerings that include institutional pressures to manage campus resources and individual faculty interest in teaching with technology, some schools may find that efforts to align learning objectives at a number of levels also lead to concentrated interest in blended learning.

Many institutions of higher learning have adopted language in their mission and/or vision statements, for example, that reflects an interest in innovation and the use of technology in course design and delivery. Indeed, the rhetoric of innovation often provides ideal language for making the highly visible or public language that institutions use to present themselves to the wider community that much more attractive.

For example, read the public mission, vision, and goals statements at Mt. San Antonio College, Santa Monica College, and Palomar College (the schools mentioned earlier as being the largest two-year institutions in the nation), and you find the following: "utilize and support appropriate technology to enhance educational programs and services"; "promote access to technology and...use technology to achieve...goals"; and, "support innovation to enhance and enrich learning environments and services."[14] Vision and mission statements are a language unto themselves: vague enough to cover a wide breadth of possibilities, conditional because forward looking, but invariably optimistic.

What really matters, of course, is how such grand ideas are operationalized for administrators, faculty, and students who live the everyday reality. In other words, what do course-specific learning objectives look like? Do the specific goals that students are to achieve and the basic competencies they are to display upon completion of a particular course reflect the larger institutional rhetoric? Even more to the point, when technology or innovation figures as part of an institution's public image, do we see these represented in specific learning objectives?

Institutional rhetoric need not align just with the specifics of classes on one particular campus, either. We might also ask to what degree institution-specific vision and mission language aligns with even broader statements of 21st-century learning objectives that are being formulated by national and international educational organizations. The argument is not that all institutions must achieve a transparent alignment from individual syllabi to the broadest of educational objectives. These latter may be so general as to become almost irrelevant for some schools. However, when institutions craft vision and mission statement language that includes appeals to classroom innovation and professes belief in technology in the curriculum and when those institutions do seek to connect their public image to broad, national learning objectives and to the everyday classroom reality that unfolds for teachers and students, blended learning becomes an especially attractive learning mode for making this happen. In other words, blended learning can become an appealing growth area for many schools as part of living up to a public rhetoric that declares an interest in technology and innovation.

Where do we find learning objectives in their broadest, most publicly visible manifestation? We have already noted one organization with a broad focus on teaching and learning: the Association of American Colleges and Universities. The AAC&U has laid out what it believes to be crucial learning goals for the new millennium through its LEAP initiative, "Liberal Education and America's Promise."[15] The "essential learning outcomes" as identified by the AAC&U include gaining skills in areas such as "inquiry and analysis"; "critical and creative thinking"; "information literacy"; and "teamwork and problem solving."[16] The focus is on higher-order thinking, especially critical and creative thinking, with particular emphasis on collaboration.

By incorporating technology into the teaching and learning experience, faculty can be part of achieving very broad institutional goals or at least of realizing in some practical way the public rhetoric that informs so many mission and vision statements. And, when institutions live up to their public language in this way, they are also realizing much broader calls for re-imagined educational goals that respond to 21st-century realities. The hybrid model may prove an ideal tool for innovation—for meeting the challenge of one's public rhetoric—without causing us to lose sight of the basic requirements we are asking students to meet in individual classes.

As is often the case, we find that preserving some of the face-to-face time of traditional classroom interaction while improving the academic experience through technology presents what seems like the best of both worlds that many believe to inhere in the blended model. Especially when institutions are eager to present a public image that embraces innovation and technology and when institutions are equally concerned to take up the challenge of learning goals that reflect our changing, 21st-century landscape, hybrid learning is an appealing option, just as it is when institutions are faced with basic problems like limited classroom space.

Perhaps more than any other issue, however, it is the challenge of improving student retention and success that may motivate institutions to aggressively explore new delivery models, like blended learning, as a way to ultimately increase the number of students who complete classes and earn a degree.

IMPROVING STUDENT RETENTION, SUCCESS, AND COMPLETION

"Universities lose money when students quit."[17] When it comes to retaining students, the fundamental institutional economics are hard to ignore. And these economics, as the most intractable within a combination of many factors, may be exactly what push institutions to become more and more interested in hybrid learning as a potential solution to poor student retention.

Retention, along with related issues of student success and completion, receives no small share of academic study, policymaker attention, and wide public discussion. Perhaps this comes as no surprise when we consider just how distressing are retention and success numbers nationally. For example, ACT, Inc., provides ample data on student retention, and one recent report indicates that just 65.9 percent of college freshman persist to a sophomore year. That means that a third of all freshman students drop out. In some cases, retention is substantially worse.[18]

We will look in chapter 3 at retention issues specific to online or e-learning, but a brief, more general discussion of retention is useful in helping us to understand just how fundamental the problem is. Ormond Simpson, a senior lecturer in institutional research at The Open University, states the fact that many schools know firsthand all too well: "the cost effectiveness of retention and financial benefits to the institution are increasingly obvious."[19]

At its most basic, the question confronting many schools is this: of the number of students who sign up to take a class, how many actually complete it? What matters for educators, of course, is not simply the number of students who pass a class but rather the number who complete a course having successfully met the learning goals for that class. Students should ideally complete a given course having truly learned basic skills and competencies. A high completion rate is not necessarily news for celebration if there happens to be an inordinately high number of low—but passing—grades. This represents completion, but only of a sort.

ACT, Inc., which provides assessment and research information to those in the education and workforce development fields, reports that the national first- to second-year retention rate for two-year public colleges is 53.7 percent. The highest first- to second-year retention rate is reported for private, Ph.D.-granting institutions. And that retention rate—the highest for any type of college or university that ACT studies—is still only 80.5 percent. The retention rate reported for four-year public colleges is 72.9 percent.[20] The national persistence-to-degree rate for two-year public colleges is 29.3 percent. Notably, the rate for degree completion for those at two-year schools in two years is 14.6 percent.[21]

The ACT, Inc., report, *What Works in Student Retention,* indicates that two-year colleges are more likely than their four-year counterparts to cite student characteristics, rather than institutional characteristics, as contributing most significantly to retention.[22] These data likely reflect the broad diversity of students attending two-year schools, not to mention the tendency for open admission schools to attract underprepared students. And, while variability in student preparedness and background should not preclude us from focus on changing institutional practices to improve retention, it should remind us that curricula cannot always follow a one-size-fits-all model, since institutional and student differences can be marked across a range of organizations.

Ultimately, the constellation of challenges that includes strained campus resources, emerging 21st-century learning objectives that are being embraced within individual departments and institutions, not to mention the statistics that indicate a real crisis in student success and retention, coalesce to form a context that is ripe for innovation, a context for hybrid learning to gain considerable visibility and traction.

So, given the potential for widespread institutional eagerness to expand the use of technology in curricular design, exactly how ready are students for more and more computer-based work as part of their education?

REACHING TECH-SAVVY STUDENTS

Much is often made of the accelerating degree to which teens, traditional-age college students, and now older demographics are embracing Web-based applications, particularly social networking tools like Facebook and MySpace. M. Lee Upcraft, in his foreword to *Connecting to the Net Generation*, goes so far as to make this assertion about "those who were born after 1982" (i.e., the "Net generation"): "Technology has always been a part of their lives, and they are not intimidated in the least by technological innovation."[23]

The popularity of photo- and video-sharing applications is growing rapidly, not to mention the growing user base for applications, like Twitter, that allow users to post updates to their Web pages on a minute-by-minute, almost a second-by-second, basis.[24] "It is obvious," writes Diana Oblinger, in "Growing Up with Google," that students of the Net generation have "integrated technology into everything they do, essentially putting their lives on the internet."[25]

This life-on-the-Web is emerging in sometimes surprising ways, and not only for the Net generation. An interesting Twitter moment came in December 2008 as part of an incident at Denver International Airport. A Continental Airlines 737 slid off of the runway, and, famously or infamously, Twitter user Mike Wilson (whose Twitter alias is "2drinksbehind") used his mobile phone—from within the plane—to update his Twitter page, communicating that he had just been in a plane crash. As the event was unfolding, Wilson publicized news of its happening.

His tweet included a string of expletives followed by, "I was just in a plane crash!"[26] This was the first public word of the event. Journalists were already beginning to understand the implications of this kind of immediacy, however, and had turned to Twitter during the attacks in Mumbai, India, that occurred in November 2008, for updates from those who were ostensibly living the experience as it happened. Most major news organizations themselves now have a presence on Twitter. CNN, for example, had, as of March 2009, more than 500,000 followers on Twitter.[27]

Witness another, slightly more mundane example of technology's penetration into everyday life: in case ordering a pizza by using the telephone seems too cumbersome and antiquated, you can now order online, even through social networking sites like Facebook, where you can find Pizza Hut's own Facebook page. "Order from Pizza Hut without Ever Leaving Facebook!"[28] Facebookers are not even ordering from the Pizza Hut Facebook site exactly, let alone from the Pizza Hut Web site; rather, users install the "Pizza Hut Interface" application on their own, individual Facebook pages. This widget—a small application that runs within another webspace—allows users to order pizza without ever leaving their Facebook page.

But is ordering pizza through your Facebook page still too slow and conventional? You could order pizza via text message instead from Papa John's. Once you register and set up a "fav" pizza on the Papa John's Web site, simply text "fav" to a special Papa John's number and your pizza is on the way. Still too many keystrokes? Well, one click of the Tivo remote gets you Domino's pizza. As NPR reports: "If you're fast-forwarding through a Domino's commercial, you'll get a prompt asking if you want to order a pizza."[29]

Many students, particularly those of traditional college age, are clearly comfortable with mobile technologies. They spend time communicating via text message, and they do much more than order pizza, all advertising stereotypes to the contrary. A 2008 Pew Internet and American Life report, "Teens, Video Games and Civics," indicates that "virtually all American teens play computer, console, or cell phone games and that the gaming experience is rich and varied, with a significant amount of social interaction and potential for civic engagement."[30] This provides yet further evidence that most postsecondary students of the near future will be comfortable with social networking and interaction via technology.

But can we assume that younger generations, statistically likely to be avid technology users, will become students who are de facto comfortable with online or hybrid learning? The answer to these questions may appear to be an obvious yes. And much of higher education is shaping its broadest rhetoric and imagining innovative technology use on the basis of this assumption.

However, from an educational perspective, we should be especially careful not to assume that students who are immersed in technologies of one kind will necessarily have an immediate facility with technologies of another kind or even with familiar technology when it is deployed in a new way. That is, the student who text messages constantly, and at lightning speed, will not necessarily have success in an online course administered through a course management system (CMS) like Blackboard or WebCT.[31] The student who maintains a vibrant Facebook page and who interacts virtually with multiple individuals and groups may not experience the same excitement when faced with an online class discussion board. In fact, though Oblinger, among many others, observes that "technology is an integral part" of many students' lives,[32] less has been said about exactly why students, and everyday technology users generally, immerse themselves in social networking and other similar online applications.

For many, social networking and communications technologies offer a convenient way to communicate with a large number of people in relatively little time. So, if convenience and ease are what users are looking for, it should really come as no surprise that traditional pedagogical goals involving considered reflection and sophisticated, formal language use fall flat when they are enacted through technology. Indeed, one might say that generally tech-immersed students will be less likely to flourish in certain online settings, not because these students do not understand how to use the technology but because the context is requiring of them an approach to technology that runs exactly counter to how it normally works best in their lives. Instead of speed and ease, students are asked for patience, time, focus, and reflection. Tech-savvy students are the least likely to succeed in the online and blended environments: it appears at first blush counterintuitive, but only if we adhere to oversimplified notions of how technology figures into daily life.

Consider a little further the case of an application like Twitter. What appeals to many Twitter users is exactly what educational applications of technology do not often invite: short, informal, surface-level declarations of the I-am-doing-this-right-now variety. Twitter updates, tweets, are often unconnected one from the next. Sometimes, the only thread that links a day's worth of tweets is that they have all been posted by the same person.

Further, Twitter posts are limited to 140 characters. Not 140 words. 140 characters. That is brevity as the soul of wit beyond what Shakespeare's Polonius could have imagined. Rarely do educational settings invite this kind of brevity. A banner that appeared on the Twitter front page one day perhaps explains it best: "stay connected through the exchange of quick, frequent answers to one simple question: What are you doing?"[33] Here, for example, is a series of tweets posted by a

Twitter user over the course of a day. The material in square brackets indicates the time and method of each Twitter post:

my book is an adventure/fantasy/non-fairy tale fairy tale for young children and old children too. there are lots of animals in it [posted about 16 hours ago from web]

claire scully, jen lobo, kate wilson, hadley hutton and janaki lennie are all cool new finds, but there are a million more that i love [posted about 16 hours ago from web]

i got the war child cd, pretty cool covers, had choice paralysis...now home drinking tea and write for an hour or so...inner thighs kill [posted 2:45 PM Mar 15th from web]

Went to the farmers market, bought juice and wildflower honey, now scanning the shelves of amoeba for some good records [posted 12:07 PM Mar 15th from TwitterFon].[34]

Notably, this last was posted from the user's cell phone. Clearly, the stated purpose of Twitter, and the manner in which most users take advantage of the application, is to provide short, more or less factual updates about the progress of their daily lives and the quick, often random movement of their minds from one thought to the next. There is no motivation for deeper reflection and literally no room, given the 140 character limit, for more sophisticated language.

There is nothing inherently wrong with this forced brevity. Twitter users do not complain about the 140 character tweet limit. In the case of users tweeting from within a major event (like Mike Wilson posting to Twitter during a plane crash), Twitter clearly has broad cultural value. Indeed its use often involves serious ramifications. For example, a Twitter user who posted the whereabouts of police during a G-20 protest event in Pittsburgh was later charged with "hindering apprehension or prosecution, criminal use of a communication facility and possession of instruments of crime." The FBI even raided the user's home.[35]

The point is less about one specific technology, however, and more about understanding how and why technology is being used by people generally. We must be careful about extrapolating from widespread technology trends to technology specifically as a feature in higher education. So, yes, many college age folks use Twitter and Facebook on a regular basis. But to presume that they will thus do well as e-learners—the logic just does not hold up.

Equally problematic in terms of forecasting student success in blended environments remains the text-dependence of so much on-line delivery. Most faculty are comfortable in the world of written communication, the purely text-based expression of ideas. No wonder that, too often, online content is provided to students in textual pieces that are much better suited to printed books than to the screen. Many students are simply "more at home with images...than text—the opposite of what most educators consider their comfort zone."[36] Carie Windham, a graduate of North Carolina State University, has noted that "Net Gen learners are more likely to respond to visual images than a form of straight text."[37] Windham does not pretend to speak for all students her age, but she likely speaks for many.

Perhaps the positive implication for educators is that if students (current and future) are comfortable with certain kinds of technology-based activities, then we have the opportunity through informed course design to take advantage of what might be students' considerable degree of existing familiarity with applications that involve social interaction online. Educators might call this interaction a form of collaboration, even if students themselves do not. Further, while statistics do not tell us about students' finesse with Blackboard per se, they certainly do indicate an eagerness on the part of young students to use technology to communicate with one another, to pool knowledge, to form groups based on shared interests and affiliations, and to shape and share often multiple personal identities and narratives with others. The question is thus ultimately about whether online learning, as part of an entirely online class or as part of a hybrid class, is incorporating elements of collaboration, collective knowledge and identity building, and group networking that students—statistically speaking, at least—seem to be interested in and comfortable with.

UNDERSTANDING STUDENTS, TECHNOLOGY, AND WRITING

Related to the issue of whether frequent technology use outside the classroom might—or might not—translate into success with technology inside the classroom is the disconnect that many students experience between the kinds of writing activities they often engage in as part of their frequent Facebook use or communication via instant message (IM)[38] with friends and the writing assignments that they are required to complete for school. According to a Pew Internet and American Life report, 73 percent of teens indicate that their daily instant messaging activities, e-mailing, and social networking actually have no impact on their school writing.[39]

Despite the fact that a majority of students do not see their writing activities outside the classroom as connected to their in-class work, many commentators identify exactly this connection. One hears the common complaint, for example, that students today cannot write. This perceived deficiency is often blamed on activities, like frequent instant messaging, that have degraded students' ability to communicate extended arguments in rhetorically sophisticated prose. James H. Billington, the 13th Librarian of the U.S. Congress, speculates, for example, that electronic communication might be causing "the slow destruction of the basic unit of human thought, the sentence."[40] Equally scathing have been comments by University College of London English professor John Sutherland: "Texting is bleak, bald, sad shorthand which masks dyslexia, poor spelling and mental laziness."[41]

The problem of poor writing carries over into the workplace. A study conducted by the National Commission on Writing suggests that corporations spend some $3.1 billion yearly on remedial writing training for new and current employees (notably, $2.9 billion of the $3.1 billion total goes toward [re]training current employees, not those hired fresh out of college). The commission's report estimates that a third of employees in blue-chip companies in the United States write poorly.[42]

However, students in my experience are rarely deficient writers because of their frequent instant messaging. If anything, students are not sufficiently conscious of writing situations and how variable they can be. What style, tone, and format is appropriate and when? In other words, too many students do not realize that writing outside of the classroom setting is still writing.

So where is the disconnect? We know that teens and young adults are writing, in some form, on a daily basis. "Writing, Technology, and Teens," a 2008 Pew Internet and American Life report, indicates that "the vast majority of teens have eagerly embraced written communication with their peers as they share messages on their social network pages, in emails and instant messages online, and through fast-paced thumb choreography on their cell phones."[43] But they enter the workforce and cannot communicate? Is this simply a generational problem that will fix itself in time? Likely not.

The solution to this seeming disjuncture certainly cannot depend solely on educators, secondary, postsecondary, or otherwise. But since the focus here is blended learning as a mode that might take advantage of technological inclinations already in evidence for large groups of students, we might actually see an opportunity to connect the dots between the digital, extracurricular writing that many people seem to be doing, the general lack of awareness that this really is writing and is thus connected to more sophisticated kinds of communication, and the opportunity that blended learning presents for educators to re-see curricular design in such a way that we invite some of those extracurricular writing habits into the classroom, physical and virtual.

If those out-of-class habits come in, perhaps we increase the chance that in-class habits will travel out, as well. Since the Web is becoming an increasingly interactive and collaborative medium, the likelihood is that people generally will become more frequent writers, even while they may not think of themselves as such when the writing situation is not a formal or traditional one. Blended learning provides the ideal setting in which students can experience and reflect consciously on writing as an activity that requires constant attention to situation. The more writing situations that students experience, the more aware they become of what is appropriate and when. Ideally, fewer students will adopt their instant-messaging style when the situation calls for much more sophisticated and formal prose. And improved student awareness when it comes to writing situations means less of the common complaint that students today just can't write.

Undoubtedly, though, some of those writing situations will be a far cry from the traditional college essay. We are much more likely to see collaborative writing as a norm. In "Imagining the Internet: History and Forecast," a number of prominent technology experts were asked to voice their "most fervent hope for the future of networked technologies." The results were revealing.[44] Almost all expressed the hope that technology will mean greater social collaboration and connection for a greater number of people across the globe. For example, Betsy Book, director of product management at Makena Technologies, which is responsible for the multiuser virtual environment *There*, said of the future of networking technology: "It's about connecting people from different backgrounds and ensuring that they have a space to come together and form friendships that last a lifetime."[45]

It finally seems obvious that higher education should be concerned with online and hybrid course design that embraces what we already know about technology users—their general preference for social networking and communications tools—and that connects their informal writing (like IMing and text messaging) with the more formal writing that is taught in school. And yet, as obvious as these concerns may seem, how often does e-learning design gravitate away from the technology tools that the majority of people use on a daily basis, presuming, it seems, that students' facility with one technology will mean facility with all technology? How often do online and hybrid offerings ignore the social and collaborative aspects made possible by the Internet in favor of models that resemble self-paced, correspondence education rather than engaged, dynamic learning?

A fundamental problem is suggested in the 2008 *Horizon Report:* "the gap between students' perception of technology and that of faculty continues to widen."[46] Many students use social networking applications, like Facebook, while significantly fewer faculty members do so. A Pew Internet and American Life report indicates that "Internet users ages 12 to 28 years old have embraced the online applications that enable communicative, creative, and social uses."[47] The older the demographic, the less likely it is for Internet users to be involved in the social aspect of the Web. The challenge that may present itself more and more visibly, for more and more faculty, will involve the professional (re)education it takes to build online components into courses that tap into students' existing technology skills and inclinations, instead of actually running counter to them.

ASSESSING THE DIGITAL DIVIDE

With skyrocketing growth in demand for and offerings of college courses that involve an online component has come the persistent problem of access to technology—what has been called the digital divide.[48] Of course, access—to education and to information—is an issue that long predates the migration of technology into education; however, the problem is perhaps acute right now because technology can be a costly addition to learning. We can expect the digital divide to remain a highly visible issue as blended learning grows. And as we will see, institutions may actually find themselves in the difficult position of deepening the divide, an unintended consequence of efforts to make hybrid learning as effective as it can be and to market it as ethically as possible.

For classes delivered entirely online, students should ideally be working from their own computers, though some students will inevitably try to use computers and Internet connections available at places of employment or even at computer labs on the campus where they otherwise physically attend classes.[49] Institutions that offer online courses and programs invariably provide guidelines for those interested in taking online classes; these guidelines delineate minimum technical requirements. The COD Online Web page suggests that students "will need regular access to a computer, be it at home, on campus, or in a public facility."[50] This echoes the language provided by the Illinois Board of Higher Education in its list of questions for students interested in online courses: "Do you have reliable access to a computer and the Internet?"[51]

Quantitative data suggest, however, that students often fail online because they have taken on too much in terms of work, school, and family commitments. Indeed, students often opt for the online delivery mode because it offers greater flexibility than traditional classroom-based classes. If flexibility is paramount, it is obviously counterintuitive to then become dependent on computer access at an institution or workplace that is not open 24/7 and at which access to a computer is dependent on the number of other users there at the time. E-learning programs, through their Web presence, through print advertising, and through direct mailing to students, would do well to state as strongly as possible—even to require—that students considering online delivery have dependable access at home to a computer and the Internet through a high-speed connection. This requirement would most likely improve retention, although it is exactly the kind of prerequisite that will exacerbate problems of equitable access.

As course components that are delivered online as part of strictly online or blended learning models begin to include more media-rich utilities, such as audio and video, online learners will require a computer—and an Internet connection—with increasingly robust capabilities. Unfortunately, many online programs do a poor job of alerting students to the potential hardware requirements for online courses. Look to the "Software and Hardware Recommendations" on many school Web pages and you may still find reference to a minimum Internet connection speed of 56 kbps dial-up modem. A high-speed connection may be recommended rather than required.[52] For example, the "UMass Online" program at the University of Massachusetts requires students to "have at least a 56 kbps modem," though "DSL or Broadband Cable [is] recommended."[53] And this is for students who may complete an entire degree online, not just a few individual courses.

Students taking an online class should be required to have access to the Internet through something other than a dial-up connection, but there is nothing in the technical requirements for many online programs that mandates a fast Internet connection. A student with a dial-up connection, asked to watch even a short video for class, could be waiting at the computer for hours. This is obviously a recipe for failure. The technical requirements issue and the related issue of access of course figure as part of hybrid and blended learning when a significant portion of the course is taking place online.

But not all students have easy access, if any access at all, to even that most basic requirement for online success: a broadband Internet connection. Students in rural locations—ironically, those who could benefit the most from distance education—are at a marked disadvantage when it comes to Internet connection speed. A Pew Internet and American Life study reports that by the end of 2005, "24% of rural Americans [had] high-speed internet connections at home compared with 39% of urban and suburban dwellers."[54] In its "Home Broadband Adoption 2008" report, the Pew Internet and American Life Project notes that "38% of those living in rural American [sic] now have broadband at home, compared with 31% who said this in 2007." And further,

"By comparison, 57% of urban residents have high-speed connections at home now and 60% of suburban residents have such connections."[55] Technologies, including wireless and satellite-based Internet access, may help to lessen the gap between urban/suburban and rural Internet accessibility; however, a significant gap still remains.

The Organization for Economic Cooperation and Development has noted that "Broadband connectivity has improved but significant divides remain between rural and urban areas."[56] The access gap between urban and rural plays out in many other ways, as reported by the Pew Internet and American Life Project: home access to a high-speed Internet connection is relatively low among the poor, the nonwhite, and the elderly. Traditionally disadvantaged populations find themselves in a familiar position when it comes to Internet access.

One possible source of dramatic change in wireless penetration involves the use of white space for providing wireless access. White space is the bandwidth between digital television channels; this space will become available as television broadcasters begin to go digital.[57] Ben Scott, the policy director for Free Press, a digital rights group that strongly supports opening white space for wireless use, has stated, "We urge the FCC to move forward with policies that will increase competition and innovation, paving the way for this revolutionary new wireless marketplace."[58] Free Press, along with the Electronic Frontier Foundation, has argued that using white space for Web access will substantially increase broadband availability. In fact, FCC chairman Kevin Martin proposed a plan to auction available bandwidth; the winning bidder would then be required to offer free broadband service to 50 percent of the United States within four years and 95 percent of the country within 10 years.[59] Wireless broadband carriers like AT&T, T-Mobile, and Verizon do not support the plan, however, and represent a powerful lobby in Washington.

Given the many competing pressures and powerful forces at work with regard to extending broadband Internet access across the nation, it may seem that the digital divide will remain a major issue for online learning, whether that learning is part of an entirely online course or just the online component of a blended class.

However, studies of broadband penetration tend to aggregate numbers for a range of demographics. In some cases, age demographics are not considered at all, which is significant for discussions of access and the digital divide with regard to higher education. We must be careful to consider broadband access as it is likely to be available for particular student populations. The degree to which access across a wide range of age demographics is significant obviously depends on the demographic that an individual institution tends to serve (or to which it hopes to be able to market itself). In other words, assessing digital-divide issues best happens institution by institution, with specific attention to the demographic that is served by each institution.

Generally, given the rapid growth in access in both rural and urban areas of the United States and the possibility that newer technologies will provide access more easily and more cheaply than has previously been the case, the problem of the digital divide is likely to become less and less acute, at least in the area of higher education. In fact, as of April 7, 2009, the FCC has been working on a yearlong initiative—a national broadband strategy—to bring broadband Internet access into every American home. Acting FCC chair Michael Copps describes the plan as "the biggest responsibility given to the FCC since the Telecom Act of 1996."[60]

Is there still a digital divide in America? Yes, clearly there is. But where it seems reasonable to do so, given the student population(s) that an institution is serving, statements that require e-learners of all kinds to have a computer at home and high-speed access to the Internet should be made as clearly as possible. This applies to students in hybrid and blended classes, even where efforts to grow such course offerings are in their nascent stages. It is precisely in these early phases of hybrid course development that strict and highly visible technical requirements may be most necessary but also when they may seem most like barriers to growth.

CHOOSING A DIRECTION

Online learning, with its dependence on Web-based communication and interaction, may seem likely to exacerbate problems of access and equity, especially as the components within courses delivered online become more robust. Further, retention and success rates, which are already precipitously low in some traditional face-to-face cases, appear even worse for online learning, as we will examine in the following chapter.

By the same token, however, we hear calls for technology to play a greater and greater role in postsecondary learning as the 21st-century educational ideals of information and media literacy, and of collaboration become ever more important. We also, of course, see a student population across higher education that is more and more likely to be made up of frequent technology users.

Does this context, including the various challenges facing higher education previously outlined in this chapter, seem inevitably to point to blended learning as an obvious solution, one to which all kinds of institutions will gravitate? Will going hybrid be the answer for higher education across the board?

CHAPTER 3

Going Hybrid: The Bigger Picture

Seeing the bigger picture when it comes to going hybrid involves first understanding a few issues that are otherwise associated primarily with strictly online learning, for we have noted that, while hybrid learning may have ancestry in a number of delivery models, its most obvious relative remains online learning. Our concern is ultimately to see how blended learning might figure as a response to continued growth in demand for online learning opportunities despite substantial evidence that indicates less than stellar results for many online learners.

Why have we seen such dramatic growth in online course offerings over the past decade? There are a wide variety of reasons, from economics to pedagogic innovation. From an institutional perspective, there is, most obviously, the considerable tuition generated from online delivery—the potential market, or customer base, expands to include anybody with a computer and Internet access. Further beneficial for the institutional bottom line is the potentially low cost incurred in offering an online course, relative to offering that same course in a brick-and-mortar classroom: pay a part-time worker poverty-line wages to administer, as opposed to really teach, a prepackaged course with no overhead for classroom space, office space, supplies, and so on. This is the worst-case scenario, at least from a pedagogical perspective, though it is happening more and more often across higher education.

A less obvious but no less important motivator for growing on-line offerings has been the effort on the part of many institutions to diversify course offerings. This might include not only developing entirely new courses in alternative delivery modes but also migrating existing classroom courses to new delivery models. For example, Habley and McClanahan report that, in an ACT survey of two-year colleges, respondents indicated that institutional factors contributing to student attrition included "Number and variety of courses offered."[1] According to respondents, this factor had the third greatest effect on attrition, behind only "amount of financial aid available to students" and " student employment opportunities." A close fourth and fifth were "student engagement in the classroom (active learning)" and "academic advising."[2] The development of online classes has provided many institutions with at least one ready response to problems of retention and attrition. The development of online courses certainly increases the variety of delivery modes available to students, if not the actual variety of courses offered. Online courses can also increase the number of sections of any given course being offered without stressing physical campus resources as would offering more of those same courses in the traditional face-to-face mode.

But incredible growth in online course offerings has, at least from the teaching perspective, much more to do with engaging students and improving the learning experience than it does with the institutional bottom line. We thus begin to see how questions about growth in online learning at some point also become basic questions about technology, since it is not so much the learning mode itself as the activities that are taking place in that learning mode that will affect the student experience. Broadly speaking, then, is there something about the technology component of distance learning that has been driving growth in online offerings and that has been drawing more and more students and teachers to the e-delivery option?

ROOM FOR INNOVATION

Certainly, many educators have realized that technology can help them to reach important educational objectives, especially where these objectives are reflecting a new awareness of our highly mediated and technology-rich culture. For example, the National Council of Teachers of English (NCTE) has asserted that "21st century literacies" should figure as a key component in college education. In a position statement of February 15, 2008, the NCTE argued that "as society and technology change, so does literacy." And, "because technology has increased the intensity and complexity of literate environments, the twenty-first century demands that a literate person possess a wide range of abilities and competencies." Today's literacy, as the NCTE envisions it, will focus not just on the use of network technologies to retrieve and consume information but also on the active creation of digital content. The NCTE position statement highlights collaboration and content creation: "Twenty-first century readers and writers need to…[b]uild relationships with others to pose and solve problems collaboratively [and] [c]reate, critique, analyze, and evaluate multi-media texts."[3]

Often, learning objectives that are generated by national organizations also coincide with forward-looking analyses that consider cultural trends broadly across education and workforce frontiers. For example, the 2008 Horizon Report, produced by the New Media Consortium and the Educause Learning Initiative, looks at what emerging technologies are likely to have a significant impact on "learning focused organizations."[4] Viewpoints in the report are drawn from an Advisory Board that features membership not only from the field of education but also from business and industry. As we think about institutional learning goals, it remains important to consider larger cultural trends in relation to emerging technologies, not to mention the kinds of workplace skills that students will need as they leave school.

The Horizon Report looks at technology that is likely to gain significant traction over three different adoption horizons: (1) within the next year; (2) within two to three years; (3) within four to five years. The link between each of the technologies discussed in the report— whether their adoption horizons are near or far—is the potential they provide for collaboration and participatory media creation. Practices enabled by emergent technology that have been evident in all of the 5 Horizon Reports since their beginning—these are called metatrends— involve the "collective sharing and generation of knowledge." A resultant metatrend is "the shifting of content production to users."[5] The key emerging technologies discussed in the 2008 Horizon Report include "grassroots video and collaboration webs"; "mobile broadband and data mashups"; and "collective intelligence and social operating systems."[6]

The capacity for technology use in individual classes to reflect these broader goals and possibilities will depend in large measure on the degree to which innovative teaching and learning are fostered and rewarded on all institutional levels, from administration to faculty to staff. "Experimentation," asserts the Horizon Report, "must be encouraged and supported by policy."[7] Too often, an institution's public rhetoric about innovation may not play out in the practical matters involved in supporting true innovation. As many faculty members have perhaps experienced, for example, proposals to modify existing syllabi to include new technology, or to use technology in new ways, can meet with resistance from administration. Equally, individual faculty members looking to incorporate new technology into their teaching can feel resistance from colleagues who are skeptical of the value of technology. And, perhaps most important, even in situations when resistance from administration or colleagues is absolutely minimal, there can remain the perceived problem of resistance to technological innovation. In other words, proactive measures on the part of an institution—by removing barriers to innovation—may be needed to truly foster cutting-edge teaching. If the perception exists that change of any kind, let alone revision to include nontraditional teaching approaches, will simply mean more paperwork, more individual planning sessions with administration, and, ultimately, the need to defend one's innovation repeatedly and at length, then that innovation is unlikely to happen on a significant scale or in a timely fashion.

The Horizon Report further asserts that "the academy is faced with a need to provide formal instruction in information, visual, and technological literacy as well as in how to create meaningful content with today's tools."[8] It makes sense that, to learn about what new media and technology can enable, students should be active users of such media and technology. They should ideally be positioned as active creators of content, not merely as passive consumers. Facing this reality, institutions are likely to benefit more and more from what hybrid course design can accomplish in terms of welcoming newer technologies into the teaching and learning environment. Notably, the benefit that the hybrid model has over its entirely online counterpart, at least relative to newer or more complex digital applications, is that preserving face-to-face contact makes it possible to work with much more high-tech utilities, since the opportunity to provide real-time, face-to-face technical explanations to students still exists. In fact, notions of what constitutes high-tech tend to be more about perception than reality. Things often seem more complicated from the outside than they actually are. And students who learn to build a wiki, for example, may feel a deep sense of accomplishment if they at first imagined such a feat to be beyond their technical skill. Educators often hear the following assertion from students, both young and old: "I'm just not a computer person." But this is rarely, if ever, the case in actuality. The computers-hate-me mindset is usually little more than unchallenged and obstructive negative self-perception.

As we have seen, though, technology for technology's sake is not the answer. In fact, introducing technology into the curriculum without attention to how or why it is deployed can produce results directly counter to what is desired. Technology, as promising as it might be for achieving important learning objectives and for improving student engagement, can actually make the problem of student success even more acute. Indeed, this seems to be exactly what has happened in the field on online learning.

RETAINING STUDENTS ONLINE: WHAT DO WE KNOW?

Interestingly, among the most common practices at two-year public colleges that are aimed at improving retention, "Instructional Use of Technology" ranks sixth among the top 15 that are cited in the report *What Works in Student Retention.* Habley and McClanahan report that 79 percent of colleges that responded to their survey indicated that technology figures as a prominent response to retention issues.[9] When technology is realized as fully online courses, though institutionally it may include much more, we see clearly the connection between online course growth and institutional hopes for improved retention.

This connection between online teaching and retention is addressed specifically in *Defending the Community College Equity Agenda.* The editors and chapter authors highlight a number of the challenges facing community colleges, pointing out specifically that "Community colleges are enthusiastically expanding online offerings and some students are gaining access to college through online education. However, many colleges focus more on the technological aspects of online education than on the educational issues that affect how well students learn the material covered in online courses." Further, "The wave of enthusiasm for distance education, especially during the late 1990s, was driven partly by anxiety among colleges that innovators and fast movers in online education would threaten community college enrollments."[10] Technology, in the form of online course offerings, seemed the ideal means to boost enrollment and to compete in a changing educational marketplace. However, an emphasis on enrollment over pedagogical soundness can compromise what Bailey and Morest call the "foundational educational activities" of a college, "teaching and learning."[11]

Retention numbers are, as we have seen, quite distressing across delivery modes. However, retention and completion numbers for online courses tell an even grimmer tale.[12] For example, in "Best Practices in Predicting and Encouraging Student Persistence and Achievement Online," authors Libby Morris and Catherine Finnegan detail their study of 400 students enrolled in online courses offered by the University System of Georgia: "Over 400 students were tracked, and slightly over 200 were successful completers."[13] These kinds of results emerge from study after study.

In her February 11, 2000, article, "As Distance Education Comes of Age, the Challenge Is Keeping the Students," published in the *Chronicle of Higher Education,* author Sarah Carr writes that "anecdotal evidence and studies by individual institutions suggest that course-completion and program-retention rates are generally lower in distance-education courses than in their face-to-face counterparts."[14] Not much has changed since 2000. A recent study undertaken by Bellevue Community College in Bellevue, Washington, sought to gauge student success in online courses. The study, "Student Success and Retention in Online Courses," revealed a number of interesting facts. First, and not at all surprising, enrollment in online courses increased significantly, more than doubling (from less than 7% to more than 14% of total enrollment), during the study period 2000–2001 to 2005–2006. Student retention, "the percentage of enrolled students who completed the course with a non-failing grade," in online courses was between 72 percent and 75 percent, 7 percent to 11 percent lower than the percentage for equivalent on-campus courses.[15]

Within-term retention rates for Spring 2007, as reported by the College of DuPage Office of Research and Planning, indicate that students in online courses fared significantly worse than their classroom counterparts. The end-of-term retention rate for online courses in Spring 2007 was 76 percent. The same rate for all academic units was 86 percent.[16]

Completion rates for disciplines within the COD Liberal Arts division range from more than 90 percent to less than 60 percent for traditional classroom delivery. Completion for English composition (not including developmental English classes) was reported as 72 percent, using Fall 2006 numbers. The total for the entire division (which is based on more than 48,000 total credit hours) is 74 percent. The total completion rate for all online classes offered by the Liberal Arts division was 61 percent, though we should note that the online rates are based on a total student count of 713, whereas the total student count for classroom classes is 17,759. The completion rate for English composition online is reported at 53 percent.[17]

It may be, of course, that comparing measures in two delivery modes (online versus face-to-face), even for the same curricular material, is ultimately an apples-to-oranges comparison and that the true measure of online success is revealed only through comparison of similar curricula offered in like delivery modes. One imagines, for example, comparing the success rates of a given student sample in a single online history class with a sample from other online history classes, not with a sample from face-to-face history classes. This apples-to-apples approach is more likely to reveal elements of course design—something that is actually within the control of teaching faculty—that may be affecting student performance.

But, despite poor retention numbers, demand for online course offerings is increasing. In fact, Wes Habley of ACT, Inc., has remarked
that "the growth of online learning has far outpaced any attempts that
I know of to conduct definitive research on its prevalence not to mention its success as a learning strategy."[18] A July 18, 2008, *Chronicle of
Higher Education* article details booming growth in online offerings for
a number of schools:

The Tennessee Board of Regents, for instance, reports that summer enrollment
in online courses is up 29 percent over last year. At Brevard Community College, in Cocoa, Fla., summer enrollment in online courses is up nearly 25 percent. Harrisburg Area Community College, in Pennsylvania, saw its summer
online enrollment rise about 15 percent. And at Northampton, in Bethlehem,
Pa., online enrollment is up 18 percent.[19]

The University of Illinois at Springfield has experienced marked
growth in online course enrollment, from 500 or so students in 2000
to roughly 4,000 as of Spring 2008.[20] And that is 4,000 students in each
term, not an aggregate total for the academic year. *Illinois Virtual Campus* reports that "there were 192,277 distance education enrollments in
11,501 distance education courses for the Spring 2008 term. This is a
14% increase in enrollment from Spring 2007 when there were 10,511
courses and 167,781 enrollments."[21] The numbers tend to tell the same
story regardless of where you look: major growth in demand for online offerings. In "Making the Grade: Online Education in the United
States, 2006," Allen and Seaman assert that "There has been no level-
ing of the growth rate for online enrollments; institutions of higher
education report record online enrollment growth on both a numeric
and a percentage basis."[22]

RESPONDING TO COMPETING PRESSURES

We thus arrive at a significant dilemma that confronts many educational institutions: how do you respond to increasing demand for
online course offerings despite evidence that indicates a much lower
student success rate for those who take online courses? As we have
noted, student surveys generally indicate that flexibility is the primary
perceived benefit to enrolling in online classes. Ironically, though, poor
retention often stems from the flip side of this flexibility: lack of regular and structured interaction with a professor and with classmates.

A number of competing pressures of this kind confront higher education: learning objectives are being reformulated for the 21st century;
technology is emerging more and more as a response to poor student

retention; online course and program growth is continuing with little sign of letting up; online offerings represent a sound financial decision for many institutions. Yet, the effectiveness of entirely online learning has yet to be proven across the board. Certainly, it can work. But does it the majority of the time?

Once again, it seems, hybrid learning finds its moment. But a fundamental problem with the development of online learning, particularly according to its detractors and skeptics, is that the forces that have motivated the continuing institutional push for more and more online options are now too mired in managerial, bottom-line thinking and rhetoric. In other words, in too many cases, and despite the best efforts of many faculty and, often, of administrators, too, online learning is inextricably more about the business of education than about the pedagogical integrity of learning and student success. When e-learning critics identify, for example, the "siren's call to e-learning" or administrations that "[prioritize] technology over people" or the forces of "managerialism and technological determinism," they are reflecting the degree to which online education has been interpolated into a market logic understanding of higher education.[23]

If hybrid and blended teaching is perhaps seeing its moment in the spotlight about to arrive—partly as a response to the various dynamics we have already discussed—we will benefit a great deal by taking care that this mixed-mode learning model does not become similarly co-opted. Therefore, rather than arguing for the hybrid model as particularly relevant right now as a response to basic institutional problems and pressures (though it certainly is such a response), we want to dig deeper in order to get at what hybrids represent in terms of technology as it is broadly conceived and deployed in our everyday lives. In other words, what might the popular media and technology landscape have to tell us about how to include technology in blended course design? In answering this question, we are broadening our notions of exactly how and why blended learning can work, how it can be pedagogically effective, beyond just defaulting to either the bottom-line logic of hybrids as cost effective (this logic now dominates the arena of online teaching and learning) or the data-driven logic of retention (itself often at root a bottom-line mode of thinking). So, before we go hybrid, we need to think as expansively and as inclusively as possible about the larger technology landscape.

OUR MEDIA-RICH ENVIRONMENT: "SHARE YOUR STORY"

The 2008 presidential campaign run by Barack Obama made the news a number of times for its interesting use of technology. For example, the campaign purchased advertising space in a video game. Players of Criterion Games' *Burnout Paradise,* a racing simulation, were likely to see advertising on a virtual billboard—either as they zoomed past it or as they flipped through the air after a crash—featuring Barack Obama and his "voteforchange" Web address.

Virtual billboard space is available for purchase in a number of video games. The advertising can be updated via Internet-connected game consoles as new advertisers jump on board. Jeff Brown, vice president of communications for Electronic Arts (Criterion Games' parent company), says that Obama's campaign bought ad space specifically for the Microsoft Xbox 360 version of *Burnout Paradise.* Brown indicates that the game appeals mostly to male players ages 16–30. The ads were slated to run until November 3, 2008, but only in certain highly contested states.[24] This selective targeting is possible through software updates, which include the advertising, that are delivered only to specific geographical regions of the country.

A perhaps more striking, if no less innovative, example of technology use during the 2008 presidential race occurred on Saturday, August 23, 2008. Then presumptive Democratic presidential nominee, Barack Obama, announced that his vice presidential running mate would be Delaware senator Joe Biden. Interestingly, the announcement came first via text message to Obama supporters (and the news also appeared on Obama's Web site). The announcement delivered via the medium of text message came well before Obama and Biden made a public statement—face-to-face, that is—in Springfield, Illinois, later that afternoon.[25] The text message included this invitation: "Please let Joe know that you're glad he's part of our team. Share your personal welcome note and we will make sure he gets it: http://my.barackobama.com/welcomejoe."[26]

The "Welcome Joe" portion of Obama's Web site provided users with a form that could be filled out with name and e-mail address. There was also space for a personal message. The invitation to e-mail a message was stated in a way that was revealing for our mediated day and age: "Share your story and write a welcome note."[27] This use of text message and Web interface provides a good example of media integration whereby content travels across multiple platforms. The rhetoric involved is also revealing of assumptions that have been made about the users of media technologies. The invitation to share your story was voiced as primary. The welcome note became secondary, despite the invitation to welcome Joe in the original text message.

What we see here is basic Web technology used to include the populace in forming the larger political narrative as it unfolds. At least, that is what the rhetoric suggests. Of course, the degree to which contributing one's story through a Web site really affects political decision making and policy is negligible, but that is not the point. What matters is that technology in this case is deployed to elicit active participation in a perceived social movement, something vastly larger than oneself but in which participation (and affective participation at that) is possible. The effect of such participation on actual policy is entirely secondary to the sense of civic participation and of grassroots community that telling one's story creates. And telling one's story, as a mode of entering the public discourse, is, in this case and in so many others, enabled by fairly commonplace technology.

The ability to be a part of a larger public narrative, part of a social discourse, is a crucial point to understand about the use of media across multiple technologies, in this particular instance. It implies a great deal that is valuable about how citizens can be made to feel empowered—part of something larger than themselves—through collaborative narrative building, or sharing one's story. What makes it work, though, is the assumption on the part of campaign planners that a certain portion of their constituency will be fluent in newer media and able (and willing) to cross media platforms, from cell phone to Web browser, in numbers sizable enough to make the strategy worthwhile. And it is this burgeoning ability to both consume and produce the larger social narrative using multiple technologies that higher education will have to grapple with, ideally sooner rather than later.

The opportunity to share one's story or to participate in shaping grander narratives actually invests the consumer with a power that heretofore has remained largely in the hands of big corporate or institutional bodies. For example, it is commonplace for companies to brand themselves with an explicit narrative, often relating the story of the organization's founding. A good case in point is the outdoor clothing retailer Eddie Bauer.[28] This retailer provides a useful example because its corporate narrative hinges so specifically on the story of an individual.

The narrative of the founding outdoorsman—of Eddie Bauer himself—is highly visible as part of the company's Web presence and often within its physical retail locations. The Eddie Bauer homepage advertises latest fashions (in rugged use, generally) but also includes an "Our Creed" and an "Our Guarantee" statement ostensibly signed by Eddie Bauer; this signature takes the form of an image at the bottom of the page.[29] The page logo, "Eddie Bauer," is also accompanied by the text, "EST. 1920." These elements imply the brand subtext: the story of Eddie Bauer himself, rugged individualist and then entrepreneur, whose personal narrative invests the corporation with a kind of humanity.

An entire timeline of Eddie Bauer's life can be found, though this interestingly shows up in the "Investor Relations" portion of the Web site. Apparently, selling the narrative is part of reaching consumers, but it is also an important part of pitching the company as unique to investors. Consumers get an eyeful of the narrative in Eddie Bauer retail stores, which often feature wall-size depictions of Eddie Bauer trekking across wintry landscapes.

Of course, consumers participate in the narrative only in that most traditional of consumerist methods: they buy stuff. Consumers buy into the narrative; they buy into the lifestyle. Eddie Bauer—the retail chain, not the man—is, of course, not alone in this kind of corporate imaging. It has become fairly standard procedure for most retailers.[30]

For example, a radio commercial for the outdoor outfitter REI—an Eddie Bauer competitor—invites listeners to check out the REI Web site to "learn the story." In fact, because REI operates as a cooperative, the sense of belonging to the community is made highly visible as part of REI's advertising. Also, as a co-op, the corporate narrative avoids the triumphant individualism of the Eddie Bauer story. According to the REI Web site: "What began as a group of 23 mountain climbing buddies is now the nation's largest consumer cooperative with more than three million active members. But no matter how large we grow, our roots remain firmly planted in the outdoors."[31] Among the usual advertising images—featuring outdoorsy, rugged, adventurous, and generally happy people—visitors to the REI homepage can find the invitation to share photos. After all, "As a co-op, REI encourages a sense of community among members and sharing photos is one way to do that."[32] REI's photo sharing is highly controlled, however, as members must submit photos to REI for screening. Users cannot simply post their own photos, as is the case with standalone Web-based photo-sharing applications. Members have, it seems, successfully submitted photos to REI; the Web site displays photos (a total of 83, as of October 7, 2008) in a slideshow format.

REI has taken the fundamental idea of a corporate narrative—which is so visibly present in the marketing and physical retail design of companies like Eddie Bauer—and has made explicit the dimension of public, or consumer, participation in the community narrative, which is exactly what we saw the Obama/Biden campaign attempting to do through its invitation to "Share your personal welcome note" with Joe Biden. However, the invitation to welcome Joe actually became, primarily, an invitation to "share your story."

It may seem that we are getting far afield of the classroom and the online educational space. But the point is precisely to bring Web and networked technologies as they are actually appearing in the popular media landscape into educational spaces in the hope of tapping into that user desire for community and active participation in the larger narrative. Why could a college course not have its own, unfolding narrative, one driven by all members of the class?

And, by seeing blended and hybrid learning in the broadest terms possible, I hope that we go at least some way to avoiding the fate that online learning has suffered: becoming so submerged in the logic of profit and loss that basic issues of pedagogy and of pedagogic possibilities get lost in the shuffle.

CONVERGENCE: TECHNOLOGY AND MEDIA PARTICIPATION

Henry Jenkins, director of the Comparative Media Studies Program at the Massachusetts Institution of Technology, has written extensively on the idea of convergence—a means of articulating the deep connections between and across multiple new media platforms and for exploring what cultural assumptions seem to underlie these media. At one point, Jenkins defines convergence as more than just "content that flows across multiple media channels." Convergence is more about the "interdependence of communications systems...multiple ways of accessing media content [and] evermore complex relations between top-down corporate media and bottom-up participatory culture."[33]

A basic example of convergence might involve television viewer participation in TV content enabled via the Web. The AMC (American Movie Classics) television channel presents viewers with the opportunity to play along with its Cinemania trivia game at home, for example. The AMC Web site describes Cinemania like this: "hardcore fans compete for the ultimate movie fan title. Each week celebrity guests join host Regan Burns to share their thoughts about the movie while posing fun, challenging questions. Fans at home will also have an opportunity to compete for a prize with an online Cinemania Quiz."[34] This is a fairly typical example of the cross-media consumer/viewer participation that is becoming more and more common.

Especially valuable for educators is Jenkins's insistence on the degree to which new media can—depending on how they are used— afford otherwise passive consumers of content the opportunity to become much more active producers of that content. As Jenkins writes of media consumption generally:

If old consumers were assumed to be passive, the new consumers are active. If old consumers were predictable and stayed where you told them to stay, then new consumers are migratory, showing a declining loyalty to networks or media. If old consumers were isolated individuals, the new consumers are more socially connected. If the work of media consumers was once silent and invisible, the new consumers are now noisy and public.[35]

Jenkins is interested in how consumers of media can be repositioned relative to media products and production not only through new communications platforms (like mobile phones and the Internet) but also through new systems of connected media (that is, a media product that maintains a presence across a variety of platforms).

This is where ideas of convergence and media participation need to be understood as part of the broad possibilities offered by hybrid learning. The opportunity presented by technology for engagement, collaboration, participation, and creative expression can be considerable. Convergence, for Jenkins, involves the (re)circulation of content (re)generated by active consumers (not customers) across different media systems. The examples that Jenkins highlights throughout his book *Convergence Culture* focus on media consumers who are taking an active, participatory role in the product being consumed. The examples of how technology, or new media, can enable participation that Jenkins presents in his *Convergence Culture* include fans of the *Survivor* television series forming "knowledge communities" and practicing a "collective intelligence."[36] In this case, devoted fans of *Survivor* attempt to identify the participant on the show who will be the sole survivor, the one contestant left after all others are voted off of the show.

The *Survivor* show goes to great lengths to guard this secret, including severe contractual penalties for show participants who divulge details before the show officially airs on television. Linked via the Internet, fans can easily pool their *Survivor* expertise to form a collective intelligence aimed at penetrating the show's primary secret. Fan groups put forth arguments for who will or will not be voted off the show. This example of a collaborative intelligence that is enabled by networked discussion boards provides a useful model for educators in that we can see the opportunity to position students not as isolated learners but as participants who both contribute to and are dependent upon a group expertise. "We are experimenting," writes Jenkins, "with new kinds of knowledge that emerge in cyberspace."[37]

According to the Web site Survivor Fever, "We enjoy bringing 'Survivor' fans all the news that's fit to print, keeping up with all your favorite contestants, past and present, but most of all, analyzing and discoursing upon each current season's episodes and contestant gameplay."[38] The ultimate draw of the television series is that it controls the release of an already completed narrative (i.e., who has won a particular season of *Survivor*) that is not entirely available to the viewer. In this sense, *Survivor* epitomizes the oldest model of media ownership. It uses corporate power, including contractual arrangements with contestants, to withhold knowledge from media consumers. Show enthusiasts, however, make every effort to wrest the secret of the narrative from corporate control. A *USA Today* article, "Internet 'Survivor' Snoops Vie to Outscoop," notes that "Internet fans are fighting back with even more resources aimed at penetrating the holy grail of television."[39] *Survivor*'s executive producer, Mark Burnett, even takes care to plant red herrings, playing his part in the game.

Another part of what is often called spoiling *Survivor*—that is, trying to know more about the show than what it officially provides—involves identifying cast members of upcoming seasons before CBS makes the public announcement and, afterwards, attempting to determine which contestants make it for how long. A typical post on a Survivor Sucks Web site forum reads like this:

I may have another lead and quite honestly, I'm surprised this hasn't been posted yet! A co-worker's friend of a friend tells me that there's a friend that had been missing in action for a few summer months and just recently returned home which happened to be the same time that production wrapped. Wide speculation among that circle of friends is that he had returned from doing Survivor because he apparently is a huge fan and had been talking about trying out. His name is **Charlie Herschel,** and he's a gay lawyer from New York City. He's a cute guy, late-20's and has done a couple of marathons I'm told. That friend said that when he surfaced back after mysteriously being away for the summer, *he was sporting a full beard. And apparently he's 'usually very clean cut.' This leads me to believe that he makes it far,* like final three at least, or maybe not...who knows? If he were in the jury, wouldn't he have cleaned up and shaved it? That's all I got for now.[40]

This prompts a post a few days later:

After finding out that Charlie was in the cast....I did a little research. I do know him on an acquaintance level and we have several mutual friends. Based on some fb [Facebook] photos of him that he posted in mid august...he is definitely still VERY tan and definitely looks skinnier than normal. I'm not going to post the pics because they are friends only....but take that for what it's worth....just another tidbit that might fuel the other info we have that suggests he made it far.[41]

Notably, part of piecing together information about cast members and speculating about how deep they go into the show itself involves checking MySpace and Facebook pages through friend connections. Social networking sites play a role, often indirectly, in media participation.

The point is not that these *Survivor* enthusiasts are necessarily right or wrong but rather that the Web allows them to practice a kind of collective thinking and speculation, pooling personal knowledge and research—the details and "tidbits"—into an often impressive (and correct, for that matter) big picture of what happens on the *Survivor* TV show. *Survivor* fan communities are able to control how the *Survivor* narrative circulates—though they do not yet control the narrative itself, unfortunately. Individuals within these communities position themselves as active and collaborative participants in *Survivor*'s media existence. This is exactly the kind of example that educators could make use of in thinking about how technology can be used to (re)position students as active learners, particularly in a blended setting that involves technology. The model of meaningful collaboration and of a collective intelligence provided by *Survivor* spoilers on the Web is deeply instructive.

Another good example of communal knowledge sharing that produces a whole that is clearly more than the sum of the parts is provided by the companion Web sites that are developed for printed books. Often advertised as secondary to their printed counterparts, so-called companion sites can in fact generate a community of users that far exceeds the number who ever purchased the printed book. Take, for example, the popular book *Baby Bargains,* by Denise and Alan Fields.[42] The book contains extensive information for expecting parents, including reviews of everything from formula to car seats to cribs. By its very nature, however, the printed book is always to some degree out of date by the time it is on the shelves.

The *Baby Bargains* Web site provides much more timely information, though for obvious reasons free content provided on the Web, at least content that is professionally authored, is fairly limited. But, while content on the site is tightly controlled so as not to make the book itself unnecessary, the *Baby Bargains* Web presence takes advantage of what the Web does much better than can a printed book: it allows for community interaction. The site provides a moderated message board, which features any number of user-created forums for questions, ideas, and discussion. This space allows registered users to post messages to any forum, asking questions of their own and responding to those posted by other users.

The *Baby Bargains* message board, called "The Baby Boards," is an ideal example of pooled experiential knowledge. The invitation to users is to "share ideas, comment on products, and get help from other parents."[43] In "The Baby Boards" forums, users share their experiences with products, good and bad, news about product sales and online coupon codes, along with parenting tips and questions. Used judiciously (i.e., what you are reading is experiential knowledge, not vetted expertise, necessarily), the *Baby Bargains* Web site may be a more effective and useful tool in the nerve-wracked world of expecting parents than is the printed book itself.[44]

In fact, the Web is more and more allowing for—and actively inviting—user input and collaboration. Where once the Web was a vast collection of static content to be consumed, it is now quite common for Web sites to include comment windows for users. The information- and opinion-heavy ESPN Web page, for example, includes a comment feature along with each of the articles posted online.[45] Articles on the ESPN site often generate substantial commentary from various participants, surpassing the original content in word count by far. After initial comments about an original news item or opinion piece appear, for example, subsequent posts often respond more to the proliferating commentary than to the original published material.

Users are also invited to create a "Fan Profile" and an avatar to represent their online identity. When you create a profile like this for yourself, you are given a limited Web presence within the ESPN SportsNation, an interesting virtual country for its various citizens who suddenly, just by signing up, have in common the same virtual nationality.[46] Your profile page allows you to provide information about your RL (real life) self (including age, RL location, occupation) and to upload a picture. Of course, you are asked to identify favorite teams.

Most notably, though—and this is the direction that so much of the Web is headed—the SportsNation site includes a message center and a groups page where registered users can search out and join groups that reflect their particular interests.[47] The applications provided by the ESPN Web site cater to an online experience well beyond just the consumption of information. Ultimately, the various tools—and the rhetoric of the SportsNation itself—invite the creation of communities of individuals with shared interests who are eager to represent themselves as virtual identities (individual and communal), learn about and identify with others, and share their own opinions. With a virtual identity, and as part of perhaps multiple virtual groups, users can comment on the content provided through the site itself and on the commentary offered by other users, citizens of the virtual nation. The possibilities that are provided by Web tools for comment sharing, identity creation, and group networking are worth paying attention to for educators. They ideally need to inform how we envision what the online portion of hybrid learning might include.

These kinds of collaborative Web tools have also had an impact on the academic community itself, as is evidenced by the number of academic venues that now provide commenting features similar to those available to the ESPN SportsNation. Where responses to published articles and commentaries once involved writing (and publishing) an entirely new text, Web 2.0 applications make commenting directly on online articles a possibility. This drastically alters the collection of voices made available to the academic world, since, traditionally, the time it might take to prepare and publish a print essay left many scholars out of the public dialogue, particularly scholars at teaching-centered institutions. And, while a comment posted to a published article online is not a publication in the traditional academic sense, Web-based comment features certainly provide a public outlet for a wide diversity of scholarly voices. This enables a much richer public discussion than was ever the case before.

We could cite any number of examples, but take this somewhat self-reflexive case: in the March 2002 *Chronicle of Higher Education*, Jeffrey Young published an article entitled "'Hybrid' Teaching Seeks to End the Divide between Traditional and Online Instruction."[48] The online version of this article provides a link to a "colloquy," an online discussion facilitated by the *Chronicle* Web site. Young's article generated 32 responses, which are now part of the public discussion about hybrids. The article itself is provided as background to the basic discussion questions: "How valuable are the emerging hybrid programs that blend distance education and classroom learning? What does this new type of education say about distance education and classroom-based instruction?" These questions, and Young's article, prompted a variety of responses in which people expressed a wide diversity of opinions, from outright skepticism of hybrids to enthusiastic support.

What is particularly noteworthy, beyond the range of responses themselves, of course, is the diversity of individuals whose opinions were made public by the Web medium. Input came from those who identified themselves as or with "salem international university," "Physics Instructor, Olney Central College," "San Jose City College," "Ph.D. Candidate, Walden University," "Associate Professor, Jacksonville State University," "Vice Chancellor Information Technologies," "Online Content Project Manager, Dept. of Education & Training," "English Instructor, Los Medanos College," "Institute of Educational Information Technology, South China Normal University," and the list continues. This represents a considerable diversity of academic situations. The resulting collection of public voices is made possible by the changing media that are now available to educators.

An equally relevant element of the convergence and participatory cultures that we are now a part of is fan fiction, which offers the opportunity to consumers to be direct participants in media creation, not just to be involved in how a product circulates (as is the case for *Survivor* spoilers) or to be a commentator after the fact (as in the comments to pieces published on the ESPN or *The Chronicle of Higher Education* Web sites). Of course, fan fiction is not new. People have been imagining and creating scripts for television characters and for characters out of popular and literary fiction for years. Michael Chabon notes that works by fans—what he calls "prose versions of the adventures, histories, and sex lives of characters from *Buffy the Vampire Slayer* and *Xena: The Warrior Princess*"—are "often derided or dismissed for the amateur productions they are, but the fact is that for at least the past forty years...popular media have been in the hands of people who grew up as passionate, if not insanely passionate, fans of those media."[49]

The Internet provides a new ease of access for those passionate content creators, along with the opportunity for communities to form across a wide geography. Consider, for example, a Web site like Fan-Fiction.net. This site provides authors with the space to present their creative work to anybody interested in reading it. Perhaps more important, the format allows for commentary (called "reviews") to be attached to posted fiction by anybody reading the work. And, while there is substantial new work that authors post, there is also a considerable body of true fan fiction, work that is derived from previously published, preexisting narratives. Users have the opportunity to extend or deepen the stories in a variety of genres, including anime, games, books, movies, and comics. Within each genre are titles of existing works or series into which authors can interject their new stories. And the opportunities are not limited to mass market or newer fiction, like the *Harry Potter* series (which is particularly popular). For example, authors can post work that extends the narratives of *1984*, *Lord of the Flies*, *To Kill a Mockingbird*, or *Wuthering Heights.* Options are not limited to specific titles, as there are broad categories—like "Bible" and "Vampires"—to which writers can contribute, as well.

One writer, identifying him- or herself as "5BY5IDIOT,"[50] has authored and posted two pieces of work on FanFiction.net. One of these works, entitled "Reason," imagines Holden Caulfield 10 years after the period depicted in J. D. Salinger's famous novel, *Catcher in the Rye:* "10 years after the book ends; this is how things are." Two reviews have been posted in response to "Reason." They read: "I really liked this:) It was great, and it actually makes me want to go read Catcher in the Rye all over again:) Congrats on a great piece!" and "That was a lot of fun! You captured the basic feel of Salinger's voice, though I could have done with a little more. Are there any more chapters? Thanks for writing it."[51] These reviews provide evidence for how a piece of fan-authored fiction might appeal to those in the FanFiction. net community.

Interestingly, many of the pieces posted for *Catcher in the Rye* began as assignments for classes. Many authors indicate that, since they had done the work already, they might as well post it. For example, one author writes, "Okay, yes this might be a bit strange. But, I really wanted to put something up and I just happened to have this lying around. FYI: It was an English Assignment about writing in Holden's voice." The impulse to go public with a creative effort is one that is often hard to take advantage of in a class, given the number of people who could feasibly read a student's work. And, of course, too often students have (or imagine they have) an audience of one: the instructor. Creative work imagined as fan fiction gives students the opportunity to see themselves as public authors, in addition to their being able to participate in an existing narrative. Students are able not just to study *Catcher in the Rye* as an object but to understand it from the inside, as authors themselves.[52]

Understanding technology as a means to facilitate content (re)generation (as opposed to mere content consumption) means we can see the instability—or the potential unfinishedness—of all media productions, both old and new. The director of BBC New Media and Technology has explained, for example, that digital technologies are very likely to change the "traditional 'monologue broadcaster' to 'grateful viewer' relationship."[53] In this sense, media content, once it goes public, is not fully in the control of an original producer. In fact, it is often surprising to observe the degree to which even the most established of media outlets are embracing a new participatory and customizable framework for their audiences, who are, in truth, no longer so much spectators as producers themselves.

NYTIMES GOES INTERACTIVE

Vivian Schiller, formerly the senior vice president and general manager of nytimes.com, is credited with significantly overhauling the venerable *New York Times'* Web presence, nytimes.com, such that it became much less an archive of what had initially appeared in print (accessible, for the most part, by paid subscription) and much more an interactive space in which content is freely available and in which Web 2.0 features allow users to comment on content and to customize their Web experience. As NPR's David Folkenflik reports, "under Vivian Schiller, the New York Times site added dozens of blogs and visual story telling features, such as videos and interactive charts."[54]

Take also, for example, the "mytimes," feature of nytimes.com. This free service allows users to personalize an nytimes Web page for themselves, one that features updated content that appeals to them. It is

"A free personalization service…My Times lets you create your own page with easy-to-browse updates from The New York Times and other favorite sites and blogs from across the Web."[55] One user may be interested in the latest stock quotes, the most recent crossword, and the day's weather, while another may be more interested in the day's lead stories and local coverage. Once a user registers and sets up a mytimes page, he or she can log back in and find the page updated with the most recent content available. This customizable content is a far cry from the previous, one-size-fits all (or none) Web site model.

The nytimes.com site also provides a "Video" area, which features a searchable library of video reports and stories.[56] Users can look at videos that have been most recently made available but can also sort videos on the basis of a "Most Viewed" tag. This is part of the more general nytimes.com feature that provides users with lists of and links to "most e-mailed," "most blogged," and "most searched" (i.e., most frequently used keywords in the nytimes.com search function). This "Most Popular" section reflects an increasingly visible Web-logic of shared experience that aligns with the premises of interactivity and community building.

By making material highly visible on the basis of how many other people have looked at (or for) it, nytimes.com foregrounds content according to public choice rather than internal corporate or editorial decision making. In some respects, users of the site affect the accessibility (or the visibility, at least) of content simply by viewing or searching for it. Users can further share content, so that Web site visitors quickly become content (re)distributors. A defining feature of the Web 2.0 age is the opportunity for Web content (audio, video, and/or text), be it generated by an established news organization, by freelance professionals, or by amateur dabblers, to go viral, that is, to spread without the help of expensive corporate advertising campaigns by traveling from individual to individual.

It is useful for educators to notice the degree to which going interactive has entirely altered nytimes.com. The Web site is now the nation's top newspaper Web site and the fifth most popular news site on the Web, as David Folkenflik reports.[57] The Web site was revamped to compete in the new digital age of user interaction, participation, and customization. In many ways, the Web site has responded to the demands of a new media landscape that have also presented themselves in calls for 21st-century learning goals that emphasize collaboration and communal knowledge building and that position learners as active creators (and sharers) of information, rather than as passive consumers. In fact, the transformation of nytimes.com embodies the basic paradigm shift we see across media entities, from a repository of content for which consumers pay and that they then passively consume to an open, dynamic, customizable Web experience.[58]

The question is whether online and hybrid courses include digital applications that advance the possibilities for user engagement (i.e., do they tend toward the new nytimes.com model) or whether they end up mirroring the logic of the old nytimes.com as containers of information that is to be passively received by each student/consumer.

PIRATES OF THE CARIBBEAN ONLINE: CONVERGENCE AND PARTICIPATION

Were we to choose just one example of how media convergence comes together with opportunities for a participatory culture, it might be—perhaps surprisingly—Disney's *Pirates of the Caribbean Online*.[59] The game is derived from the lucrative series of *Pirates of the Caribbean* movies, starring Johnny Depp, Orlando Bloom, and Keira Knightley. The trilogy includes *The Curse of the Black Pearl* (2003); *Dead Man's Chest* (2006); and *At World's End* (2007). A fourth film in the series is planned, for which Depp has reportedly received an up-front payment of $59.2 million. The first three films earned an astonishing $2.7 billion at the box office. In short, the franchise is big money for Disney Studios.

A massively multiplayer online role-playing game (or MMORPG) provides the ideal digital application to keep moviegoers interested in the narrative and to ultimately make some feel that they are a (virtual) part of the *Pirates* world. In this case, we also see how a media product travels successfully from one medium to another. The online role-playing environment further enables consumer participation in the franchise, though once again the consumer's ability to actually change the media product remains limited.

One game designer has suggested, however, that user feedback does play a role in continuing game improvement and development. One game developer was asked in an interview, "Do the developers actually read any of the feedback that players send in or does Customer Service handle all of that?" He replied, "Yes, we definitely do! We are constantly shaping the game according to player feedback we receive through Customer Service and from what we read on fan forums."[60] So-called Game Masters (Disney's game managers) also make appearances in the online *Pirates* world every once in a while in order to interact with players. By harnessing the power of MMORPGs for educational purposes, or at least by understanding their draw for so many users, we may be able to create learner-centered scenarios in which participants can affect change in the virtual world of which they are a part. This is not about playing games so much as it is about a deep engagement with, even a personal investment in, an online collaborative enterprise. So what does *Pirates Online* tell us about virtual interactive spaces?

Pirates Online offers a variety of subscription levels, from a free basic access package to an annual pass for $79.95. Notably, game content differs dramatically depending on whether you choose a free or a paid subscription. The Web-based portion of *Pirates* includes all of the elements users come to expect from a community, or multiplayer, application, including an FAQ, a photo album, and even a map to indicate actual player locations in the United States. The game is designed to work best when players collaborate. Developer Jason Yeung notes that "It is possible to [play] solo, but a core part of our game is the ability for players to assemble a crew of friends."[61]

On October 9, 2008, the *Pirates* development team opened the "Grog Blog," a weblog where users can post comments and interact with developers and other game players: "The Grog Blog gives players a direct line to the *Pirates Online* Crew—now you can leave comments on *Pirates Online* about new game features, ask questions, and connect with thousands of other Pirates around the world."[62] Building a community among players shares equal importance here with providing an avenue through which gamers can potentially shape the game world itself. The first "Grog Blog" participant, who goes by the name of James Ironhawk, wrote enthusiastically, "This [the interactive blog] is something I'm looking forward to. This will give us players a chance to say what we want. You developers have been doing a great job and doing this [implementing the game weblog] will make the game better [and] more fun! If you hear our ideas there could be some good ones out there that you [might just] add." Yet another player wrote, "This Grog Blog is going to be very handy giving players the ability to inject gaming options and play. Thanks for the chance to get creative with an already great game." And still another, "I feel that we the players can help to improve the game play and improve the fun for all."[63]

Almost all of the initial comments celebrated the perceived opportunity for players to influence future game development. This speaks volumes about the desire on the part of game participants to be more than consumers of the media product, more even than participants in the game experience, and actually to have creative input into the product they are consuming. And, while game developers or their corporate employers may in reality pay little attention to gamers' input, it is rather more likely that user input will affect future improvements and changes and that the sense of community building and participation is legitimately real for all involved.

Game play requires users to download and install a free application. The first step is to create a Pirate avatar. One can choose from a couple of body shapes and skin tones, along with choice of gender. Creating a face is an involved process, however, whereby one can tailor feature size and shape. There are, for example, no fewer than eight options when it comes to nose design, including "bridge width" and "nostril deform." Users can choose "randomize" to save time; however, game designers clearly believe that it will be important for players to look a certain way within the game.

The game is scripted and relatively limited to start. Your character is directed into the larger narrative and introduced to the basic mechanics of gameplay through interaction with nonplayer characters. However, as you move through the game world, you are likely to encounter other playing characters. You do have the ability to chat and to gesture, though in my experience most players are more eager, at least at first, to pursue the quest-based narrative that initiates the game. It is later possible to join crews, collaborative groups that can work together to defeat challenges in the game.

Opportunities for true collaborative problem solving are, of course, limited to what the *Pirates* game world allows. So collaboration, in my initial experience playing *Pirates* online, mostly involved being part of a crew aboard a sailing ship. One character handled the wheel, while others operated cannons on the port or starboard sides of the boat. *Pirates Online* rather quickly turned into a first-person shooting game: I attempted to aim my cannon and to fire at enemy ships as they sailed past. The more you play, however, the more interesting things become. And, if the sheer number of people playing *Pirates* online is any indicator, the initially limited collaborative possibilities are not a deterrent.

This last is perhaps a point worth emphasizing: *Pirates Online*, and applications like it, suggests the possibilities for interactive, online, and collaborative opportunities. And they reflect a general desire on the part of users for these kinds of opportunities. Proponents and detractors of technology alike too often identify technology applications themselves as likely to produce (or to hinder, depending on one's perspective) the development of certain intellectual habits. Proponents see online collaborative games as building a new kind of intelligence in players, a more adept problem-solving and analytical sense, not to mention a greater appreciation for group dynamics. James Paul Gee and Michael H. Levine have noted that "many young people today play long and difficult video games that involve complex thinking and problem solving married to complex language."[64]

Technology detractors cite the proponents' views, only to then cite testing statistics that indicate that frequent technology users (indeed, whole generations in some cases) have not developed any greater intellectual capabilities thanks to their digital immersion; rather, they have likely lost certain fundamental critical abilities, not to mention that increased screen time means decreased book time. This is the basic premise of Mark Bauerlein's 2008 book, *The Dumbest Generation,* for example.[65]

The assumption too often is that games like *Pirates of the Caribbean Online* in and of themselves have these kinds of effects, good or bad. It is much more useful to understand *Pirates Online* as a platform whose potentials could be unlocked by thoughtful and informed educators. In other words, online game play could be part of a curriculum that still focuses primarily on textbook material. Game play might accompany the reading of a novel, for example. And, of course (though this does not always seem to be the assumption), game play will be undertaken with clear educational objectives in mind; despite the potential openness of in-world game action and dynamics, the larger context of play ideally would be highly constrained, purposeful, and intentional within the educational setting.

In Bauerlein's book, *The Dumbest Generation,* he argues for the (re)assertion of professorial authority in the classroom. The professor needs to be, in Bauerlein's view, an active representative of a body of knowledge, a discipline, a tradition, rather than the facilitator that, in educational circles, seems now so prized. Bauerlein is quick to dismiss technology in education as having missed its mark. It represents, in Bauerlein's view, an enormous cost that has shown no tangible results. A middle position may be useful here: educators do need to assert themselves as intellectual leaders in a classroom by setting boundaries and defining clear expectations, providing direction (and correction) when necessary. This hardly precludes doing interesting things with popular online applications though.

In fact, the potential of many online applications (games or otherwise) may be realizable only with active professorial constraints. In other words, rules dictate what can and cannot be done, and in this sense they are what make games possible. Rules do not prohibit play; they enable it. *Pirates Online* in the classroom may be new and cool, but students will reject it as a fashionable waste of time unless it is tied to specific learning outcomes and unless its use is largely prescribed by the educator in charge. Of course, terms like "constraint" and "rules" and the idea of a professor being "in charge" are most retrograde to the often expansive, if sometimes empty, rhetoric surrounding modern, learner-centered education. But, when it comes to making online games and the like actually do something for a student, such prescription will be more and more necessary.

Pirates Online is hardly the only choice out there. Other popular games that work on a similar principle include *World of Warcraft* and *Ultima Online,* though neither offers an entirely free playing option; the best you are likely to get is a free trial period. *Ultima Online* welcomes players to "a world that offers thousands of hours of fun, adventure and community," an interesting triad that educators should be paying attention to. And *World of Warcraft* boasts some 10 million players.[66] The fact is, most video games these days offer some form of networked play, either through true network connection (players can join the game from anywhere that the Internet is available) or through ad hoc networks (local connections among a small group of physically proximate individuals). Many games work best when players work collaboratively. Often, certain game elements are available only when players team up.[67]

The point, finally, is not to infuse educational curriculum throughout with these applications exactly (though a little game play here and there might be a lot of fun) but rather to consider how many kinds of online applications can be deployed in (or maybe even developed for) the educational setting in order to tap into what emerges so clearly as participants' desires for community and for active participation in their media landscape.

In considering the bigger picture for going hybrid, what we see is ultimately a confluence of many pressures and possibilities. These include increasing interest in online learning, though data that suggest it is not always working as an effective educational delivery mode. Blended learning further becomes an ideal setting for educators to innovate and to re-envision existing curricula. We further know that technology is a key component in many educational settings, but it remains an element of education that could be more often intentionally shaped to reflect how technology is actually being deployed by successful media and entertainment outlets more generally. Given this big picture, the question of whether or not institutions will eventually go hybrid is one that needs to be addressed sooner rather than later.

CHAPTER 4

Hybrids: A Cultural Moment and Its History

Hybrid learning has yet to become a widely accepted institutional presence, though it is certainly in a nascent period. Hybrid learning does not yet share the wide institutional visibility of online learning, but it may do so very soon. As we enter what may be a period of rapid and widespread growth in blended learning, we need to see this learning model as part of a much broader cultural and historical moment. In no small way, this wider vision will help to provide a sense of the why behind hybrid course design and delivery beyond the market logic that continues to dominate the institutional imperatives that drive growth in online learning.

The idea of hybridity as a cultural imperative comes to us at an interesting historical moment. Hybridity is rarely understood as the simple combination of two (or multiple) things. Rather, hybridity as a cultural value consistently represents a nonexclusive option whereby we imagine we can have the pro of something without having to accept the con and through which we can make one choice without entirely excluding another. We are getting, we imagine, that cliché so often associated with hybrids in education and beyond: the best of both worlds.

In some cases, we might even get the best of many worlds, for hybridity does not always just mean one thing derived from two. Hybridity can just as easily connote creation derived from many sources, creation without destruction, and an acknowledgment of multiplicity without disregard for origins. In our globalized and highly mobile age, this has significant implications for individual and group identities.

In an April 20, 2008, article, political commentator Steve Rosenbaum wrote, "If you haven't noticed—we're living in the era of the hybrid.... New mixes. New cultural combinations. And with this new era of Hybrid Politics—an opportunity to see the [world] in a new way." The title of his article? "Is Obama a 'Hybrid'?" Rosenbaum's premise was that then–Democratic presidential candidate Barack Obama represented a mix of insider/outsider, a combination that made him, at least according to Rosenbaum, a strong candidate particularly for this historical and cultural moment.[1] You can take or leave the politics, but the broad cultural ideal of hybridity as a possibility is clear. If anything, hybridity is preferable to a once-prized purity. Being a hybrid means you are diverse, not insular, and that you have access to a breadth of experiences. You are not Ivy League or Joe Six Pack—you are Ivy League and Joe Six Pack. Of course, the identity politics associated with hybridity show up elsewhere, too.

The musical genre called urban desi provides another contemporary cultural example of hybridity. Urban desi describes a musical genre that brings together elements of hip-hop (primarily American), Bollywood (the Hindi-language film and music industry operating largely out of Mumbai), and bhangra (with folk origins in the Punjab region of Pakistan), not to mention influences from reggae and ska. A recent product of the urban desi hybrid includes "Singh Is King," a popular music single attached to the Bollywood film of the same name. Bollywood film and music star Akshay Kumar and American rap icon Snoop Dogg collaborated on the "Singh Is King" track. Snoop, in fact, appears in the movie, too—the first time an American rapper has shown up in a Bollywood production. In the video for "Singh Is King," Snoop is at one point pictured in a long embroidered coat and a turban, adopting a stereotypically Indian look, just as Kumar himself appears in Westernized garb (though still with a turban) and gestures in ways that recall American music video more than Bollywood cinema.[2]

Anjula Acharia-Bath, an urban desi fan and creator of www.desihits.com, arrived in the United States in 2001 "dismayed to find that the fusion of music she'd grown up with... wasn't really getting much play." According to Acharia-Bath, "for young South Asians in the West, this music culture represents a kind of freedom—not having to choose between two worlds." And she goes on, "We needed to create something that defined us and was our identity but makes us feel really good about this bicultural life that we lead."[3] In fact, Snoop Dogg is reportedly planning to tour India as urban desi cycles back to audiences in

South Asia, gaining new popularity largely through social networking sites like Facebook.

The comments of Acharia-Bath regarding identity and cultural roots speak directly to the possibilities that hybridity represents: ideally, a fusion without loss. Of course, multicultural identities are extremely complicated, and rarely, if ever, can the tensions of multiplicity be entirely smoothed. Nor, perhaps, should they be. Some urban desi fans, for example, are quick to identify inauthenticity as a kind of cultural betrayal, almost a hybridizing gone wrong. For example, Shaman Ajmani told NPR that "I do see some Indians over here [in the United States] using the N word. It's so annoying. I feel like saying, 'What're you doing, man? Don't try to be black.'"[4] What Ajmani may be identifying is that problematic hybridity in which one identity is given over to or eclipsed by another, inauthentically adopted, identity. In other words, the positive aspect of identity preservation, even in the face of creating something new, may be lost.

The article on NPR's Web site about urban desi and the collaboration between Snoop and Kumar on "Singh Is King" generated comments from listeners who heard the piece, reported by Nishat Kurwa, on the radio. The first commenter, Heidi Frey/Rastadevi, wrote, "Regarding the radio program: It's DAY-she. Not DAY-see [desi]. Ugh. PIO [Persons of Indian Origin] mistake. Big, sad, PIO mistake." Frey targets a perceived mispronunciation—of the word "desi"—by the Indian reporter as a kind of cultural betrayal, perhaps evidence, in the commenter's eyes, of a lost cultural connection and identity, as though what we are seeing is more assimilation than a successful hybridization. A subsequent commenter offers a clarification, however: "DAY-she, is the Bangla pronunciation, [in] Hindi and Urdu it's DAY-see, so NPR is quite right here."[5] In this fascinating reassertion of cultural variation, one commenter counters an earlier charge of cultural loss and betrayal. And these kinds of variations are important, since they represent the preservation of nuance and detail as crucial to positive hybridity. A hybrid that simply flattens difference or that features one element of the hybrid occluding, even controlling, the other is unproductive and dangerous.

Nowhere is hybridity as a cultural value more materially visible than in the world of automobiles, however, for here the notion of the hybrid is understood to represent a consumer choice with global repercussions. Hybridity is thus understood to have political implications and becomes a mode of social participation that responds to another great cultural imperative of our time: act locally, think globally.

And, while these kinds of far-reaching cultural imperatives may not figure directly in the rather narrow enterprise of hybrid course design and delivery in higher education, it is nonetheless valuable to understand that higher education's move towards hybridity—if, where, and when it happens—is certainly part of a larger social, global, and political consciousness. In other words, the notion of a hybrid class may well appeal to many students because the larger social imperatives of hybridity (and those implicitly linked with the idea of hybridity) are so strong and so visible. A hybrid class might make sense because it feels like a natural choice, the positive rhetoric of hybridity having penetrated so deeply into our culture.

The Toyota Prius, one of the most visible of all hybrid automobiles, first went on sale in the United States in December 1997. Not until 2004, however, did sales skyrocket, reaching 53,991, as compared to the 15,556 sold in 2001. Sales doubled from 2004 to 2005.[6] The Prius also found itself on the *Car and Driver* "Ten-Best" list for 2004. The appeal of the Prius is primarily fuel efficiency. And yet there are (or could be) much more fuel-efficient vehicles. Electric vehicles, for example, burn no gas at all, since they do not rely on an internal combustion engine. And yet electric vehicles continue to struggle for mass public acceptance, with criticism (fair or not) continuing to focus on speed, range, and actual energy efficiency once the cost of producing the electricity itself is factored in. Still, for most of the car-buying public, nothing can compare to internal combustion for sheer horse power. Many car buyers seem to have found a middle way in the hybrid. Automobile producers responded quickly to early hybrid-vehicle successes, and there are now any number of models, from an array of manufacturers, that come as hybrids.

Clearly, we find ourselves at a cultural moment that is particularly open to hybridity, as the concept of hybridity carries with it considerable positive cultural value. So the opportunity to grow hybrid offerings effectively and thoughtfully in higher education seems ideal, particularly because we can think beyond the most basic market concerns that can so envelop the broader pedagogical, even cultural, value attached to certain learning modes.

That said, however, hybrid learning is not exactly new. Hybrid learning is, at least to some degree, part of a long history of distance education. And so, while we look to take advantage of our cultural moment—and hybridity's capital—let us also think about its historical roots.

HYBRID LEARNING AS DISTANCE EDUCATION

Distance education, while today generally associated strictly with computer-based learning, actually has a long history, going back hundreds of years. For distance education to take place, all we need is a means to facilitate communication between an instructor and a student that does not require face-to-face presence. The history of distance learning has thus always been tied to advances in communications technology, including the development of first the postal system, then radio and later video communications, and now the Internet.

Isaac Pitman is often identified as an early pioneer in distance learning. He offered a course on shorthand via correspondence out of the private school he had founded in Bath, England, in 1840. In 1856, Charles Toussaint and Gustav Langenscheidt founded a school for the teaching of languages by correspondence. The Toussaint-Langenscheidt method, as it came to be known, involved printing a word in one language, beneath which were printed a phonetic pronunciation and a translation. Students received monthly letters, which contained vocabulary printed in this way. They were urged to practice pronunciation on their own and also required to send in a written assignment, to be corrected and returned by an instructor.[7]

In 1873, in the United States, the Society to Encourage Studies at Home was founded. While this organization soon failed, a Correspondence University was eventually organized in 1883, centered in Ithaca, New York. It consisted of instructors from various institutions, and its stated purpose was "to supplement the work of other educational institutions by instructing persons who from any cause were unable to attend them."[8] As was pointed out in an otherwise enthusiastic article in *Harper's Weekly* in 1883, however, the Correspondence University "is not chartered and has no authority to confer degrees."[9]

Degree-granting institutions had developed distance degrees even earlier, often as part of university extension services. In 1874, entire degrees could be earned from Illinois Wesleyan University by correspondence. Technical and vocational education by correspondence was available through the International Correspondence Schools of Scranton, Pennsylvania, as of 1891–1892 (cumulative enrollment began in 1891 at 115 and grew to 2,580,362 in 1923). And when Dr. William Rainey Harper became president of the University of Chicago, in 1892, he established a correspondence program through the university's extension service, largely a result of his much earlier experiences with education via correspondence associated with the Chautauqua movement of the 1870s.[10]

These examples, while suggesting the deep and various history of distance learning, do not in fact provide evidence of what would become the primary problem of distance learning as it moved into the 20th century. Lack of regulation, coupled with unscrupulous business practices, allowed education to be commodified and commercialized; the goal was not quality teaching or student success but rather profit.

Noffsinger estimates that "the sum of $70,000,000 [was] received annually in tuition fees" by the 127 correspondence schools that made up his study sample in 1924. "Seeing the possibilities of quick and easy profits if certain tactics were adopted," Noffsinger writes, correspondence school founders—often former salesmen, not educators—crowded into the distance education game.[11] This set the scene for education to become profitable business and thus for the logic of cost-benefit and supply-and-demand to shape instructional offerings and delivery. It is perhaps not surprising that one of the major distance learning accreditation organizations was founded at just this time. The Distance Education and Training Council was founded in 1926 "to promote sound educational standards and ethical business practices within the correspondence field."[12] It is revealing, a little alarming even, that business practices and ethics would figure here at all.

But because delivering instruction by mail required nothing more than a stamp in some cases, a brick-and-mortar campus being unnecessary in many situations, and because demand for marketable skills was continually growing, there arose the opportunity to sell an education, using the cheapest means possible, at considerable profit. Students quickly became customers, the public that wanted an education became the marketplace, and the business of education was born. We might also note that whereas Isaac Pitman began by training pupils in a very particular skill—shorthand—the field of correspondence, or distance, learning grew to encompass all facets of education, not just practical, skill-based subjects like the shorthand that Pitman taught.

A delivery mode that might have been perfectly suitable for training was not necessarily sufficient for enabling a college education, assuming that such an education involves not just learning technical skills but also developing higher-order facilities like critical and creative thinking, problem solving, exposure to a diversity of sometimes competing ideas and world views, and, crucially, the opportunity to gain self-knowledge though interaction with a diverse group of one's peers. Such interaction need not take place in a physical, face-to-face situation, but removing basic student interaction as a component of higher education is perhaps the most egregious pedagogical inheritance provided to modern, high-tech, distance learning from its correspondence-school ancestor.

And, unlike Isaac Pitman, himself an educator, author, and the founder of his own private school, not all distance educators were necessarily experts in an educational field, nor did they necessarily have students' best interests at heart. Often, for example, the feedback that was provided to correspondence students was the product of contingent labor working piecemeal, usually paid a very low sum for every lesson graded and returned. Obviously, in this arrangement the pressure to earn enough to survive competes directly with the pedagogical imperative to provide students with meaningful feedback, real commentary as opposed to mere correction or just a grade. Beyond the issue of meager pay and, of course, the untenable situation of paying on a per-lesson basis, another product of contingent labor as the profit-making backbone of early distance education is lack of educator investment in curriculum. In most cases, those who graded the lessons submitted by correspondence students had not created the course material, nor were they given input into its design or implementation. To be sure, there must have been many earnest assignment graders who, despite low pay, absent institutional support, and no curricular input, worked to provide students with useful commentary. But the position in which many of these workers found themselves was extremely difficult. This scenario provides an early example of the problems that continue to plague distance education in the information age.

In fact, the issue of curricular oversight remains contentious, as online education—when it is understood simply as a new mode of correspondence education—affords institutions and education corporations the opportunity to buy curricular content, deliver it via the Web, and hire contingent labor to manage the basic technical matters of course delivery and to assign grades. This online labor force may have little institutional support and little input into curricular design, as was the case with its correspondence-based distance learning predecessor. Pay may similarly be based on student success, this itself just a measure of how many paying customers can be ushered into, and then out of, the virtual door. Success may also reflect little else than student, or more properly customer, satisfaction, a market-logic measure that is often at odds with quality teaching.

Teacher investment in curricular design is also too often an absent piece of the Web-based distance learning puzzle, an unfortunate holdover from early for-profit correspondence learning. At many colleges and universities, for example, full-time faculty may be compensated for the development of online courses; however, those courses become the intellectual property (IP) of the institution. And while, in most cases, those faculty are designing courses that they themselves will teach, it is not uncommon to hear that faculty looking to move to the online environment are being asked or required to teach courses that already exist in a course management system, waiting to be administered for students.

Many faculty end up inheriting a course that is not theirs. As such, it does not reflect their particular interests, teaching style, organizational preferences, or tone. And, further, because of the way that canned courses are handled administratively—a first version can be treated as a master or template course, despite its having been subsequently heavily revised and improved through each semester's iteration—a faculty member may actually be receiving the pedagogically and organizationally worst version of that particular course.

The situation is even more problematic in cases where curricular development has been outsourced entirely. For example, so-called content experts may be hired to develop material that will then be assigned to contingent employees to teach. In some cases, it might be more accurate to say that these courses are delivered, administered, or managed, rather than taught. In their "Distance Education Survey—2007," the Distance Education and Training Council reports that 26 percent of respondents from postsecondary institutions, all of whom are members of the Distance Education and Training Council accreditation group, indicate that typical new online courses are "created by both in-house and outside authors." Twenty-six percent also report that new course development occurs through "published textbooks with study guides and outside authors." Unfortunately, no elaboration on the details or implications of these numbers is provided. Only 10 percent of respondents indicate that typical new courses are "created entirely by in-house staff."[13]

One can also find job postings specifically for curriculum experts/content writers. A typical ad reads, "We are currently seeking Subject Matter Experts in Business to develop and rewrite curriculum for our Online Business Management courses."[14] This contract work usually requires at least a bachelor's degree in the relevant field, but there is no promise that the developer will ever actually teach the course. And, aside from a degree in a content area, there is no indication that professional training in instructional design is necessary.

The U.S. Department of Education notes that reviewers from a number of accrediting agencies look for "appropriate academic oversight" in their evaluation of online course development. Further, "Reviewers from regional accrediting agencies look for evidence that faculty who are involved in governance have oversight of the curriculum." And if outside experts are paid to provide curriculum, "the reviewers ensure that faculty have defined course scope and objectives and that faculty review the courses after they have been developed."[15] A notable red flag for accreditation reviewers, according to the Department of Education, occurs if "procedures for approval of distance education curricula differ from those for traditionally-delivered curricula."[16]

The online delivery mode—the technology—is too often just providing a new means to carry on the profit-making agenda of the earliest (and worst) examples of distance education, degrading the educational environment for students and teachers alike. This may ultimately be driving what many commentators perceive to be the unfortunate shift in higher education toward a "narrow mission of job training and away from the more complex democratic mission of empowering critical citizenship."[17] David Noble, in his *Digital Diploma Mills,* argues, in fact, that "then as now, distance education has always been not so much technology-driven as profit-driven."[18]

Consider just one example of education as profit-driven industry: Education Management Corporation (EDMC).[19] According to its Web site, EDMC is "among the largest providers of private post-secondary education in North America, based on student enrollment and revenue, with 88 locations in 28 U.S. States and Canada." Further, "EDMC has proudly provided career-focused education for more than 40 years." The board of directors is made up primarily of equity and investment firm executives, including members from Goldman, Sachs, and Co., Leeds Equity Partners, and Providence Equity Partners. EDMC's share price, as reported on its investor relations Web page, went from a close of $4.094 on October 31, 1996, to a close of $42.980 on June 2, 2006.[20] Quite a moneymaker for those who were in on the ground floor.

What drives these earnings? How can the ideals of student success and quality instruction compete with the pressure to please investors? These are exactly the kinds of questions we would rather not have to face at all when it comes to higher education, yet they loom more and more ominously, especially as distance learning continues to represent an area of potential profit...big profit.

Consider that a major revenue generator like EDMC does not actually operate institutions that are entirely online. But when it comes to higher education and market forces, distance learning presents one clear opportunity to significantly reduce costs. So when education becomes big business—and it certainly can, if earnings like those reported by EDMC are anything to go by—online learning may look even more attractive as a profit maker: no brick and mortar required, and, perhaps more important, no need for the cost of a full-time professoriate. Rather, since the intellectual property rights of an online course often reside with the institution (or corporation) that has paid for its development, and not with the individual who actually created the course, once a course is prepared as a deliverable package, it can be taught by a part-time, contingent workforce. This workforce is rarely compensated with benefits or a retirement package of any kind, and it rarely receives permanent office space in which to work. In short, the resources that are fundamental to effective teaching and scholarship—employment stability and, literally, a place to work—are not necessarily present.

DIPLOMA MILLS: THE NEW SHAPE
OF AN OLD PROBLEM

The market pressures to which teaching with technology can respond have resulted in an abundance of unaccredited, for-profit businesses, run largely via the Web, that promise degrees but that are not, in fact, legally accredited to grant such degrees. These diploma mills are fraudulent businesses. The problem of diploma mills is compounded by the problem of accreditation mills. In some cases, fraudulent institutions claim to be accredited, but the accrediting body is, of course, fraudulent, as well. Commonly, the bogus degree granter and its accrediting body are owned by one parent company.

Diploma mills thrive in part because workplace salary schedules and opportunities for career advancement are often predicated less on actual experience than on educational attainment. One dubious-looking Web site, for "MUST High School," claims to grant high school diplomas, noting, as these kinds of sites usually do: "High school diploma holders earn almost double the annual income of those who drop out of high school."[21] There is a considerable market of individuals who want a degree, any degree, in the least amount of time and with the least amount of effort. They are interested not in an education but in documentation of some kind that will move them up the salary scale. It is hard to blame the individual in this case. The severely degraded value of an education is really the fault of compensation schemes that require a degree without attention to individual skill or experience or to the merit of the degree itself. Regardless, there is enormous demand for quick degrees, and the market is therefore ripe for fraud.

However, efforts to inform the public about diploma mills are considerable, both nationally and at the state level. For example, the Illinois Board of Higher Education provides a list of accredited colleges and institutions in the state,[22] and Illinois Virtual Campus provides a searchable database for students interested in online courses or programs offered by Illinois institutions accredited by the North Central Association, one of the six regional accrediting associations that monitor U.S. schools.[23]

The Council for Higher Education Accreditation (CHEA) also offers extensive information on accreditation and fraud, including information on diploma mills. The CHEA provides a searchable database of institutions and programs that have been accredited by recognized U.S. accrediting organizations, along with a directory of accrediting organizations themselves.[24] One hopes that even the least savvy of educational consumers will be alerted to potential fraud when text appears, on even the flashiest and most impressive of Web sites, like this: "MUST's online accredited diploma can be completed in less than a year (even lesser!)." A search for MUST's accrediting body, the "International Accrediting Organization," in the Council for Higher Education Accreditation database does not produce results.

The problem of fraudulent degrees will no doubt persist, and the educational marketplace will likely remain an enticing setting for dubious hucksters to practice their trade. However, the issue of degree fraud has become increasingly visible over the past few years. One member institution of the Distance Education and Training Council notes that "Consumers...seem to be more savvy about accreditation and research it."[25] The public is—one hopes—not so easily fooled when it comes to quick and easy degrees as might have been the case in the past.

Some recent cases of diploma fraud have also gained wide visibility. In 2004, for example, the Government Accountability Office reported that several high-level federal government employees had represented themselves as holding advanced degrees, though it turned out that those degrees were not from accredited schools. The report concludes, "[T]he records that we obtained from schools and agencies likely understate the extent to which the federal government has paid for degrees from diploma mills and other unaccredited schools."[26]

One case is particularly striking. In 2003, Laura Callahan was revealed to have received her doctorate from Hamilton University. Unlike Hamilton College (an accredited and highly selective school in New York), Hamilton University was a diploma mill that reportedly operated out of an old Motel 6 in Wyoming. Hamilton University was dismantled by court order, though it reopened as Richardson University for a while and appeared to operate out of the Bahamas. Richardson University does not currently seem to be operating at all. Callahan, however, used her degree to gain a position of considerable authority as a senior director in the Department of Homeland Security. After being exposed as holding multiple degrees from an unaccredited school, Callahan resigned, though she was never charged with any crime. Indeed, only fairly recently, in 2002, did the Homeland Security Act amend section 4107 of the U.S. Code, "Academic Degree Training," to allow federal reimbursement only for degrees earned from accredited institutions.[27]

Sometimes the problem is not even outright fraud. Consider an example like the University of Northern Washington (UNW), which is unaccredited but open and forthright about it. The UNW Web site advertises that their "intensive, fast-paced degree programs are best suited to the professional already working in the field of study"; further, UNW provides "[r]ecognition of self-taught learning and of skills acquired through on-the-job experience and training."[28] The target market is explicitly the adult student who is already part of the workforce and requires a degree for promotion or movement on the salary scale. The UNW "Accreditation" Web site is quite clear, and the capitalization is theirs: "THE UNIVERSITY OF NORTHERN WASHINGTON IS NOT ACCREDITED BY A RECOGNIZED ACCREDITING AGENCY OR ASSOCIATION RECOGNIZED BY THE UNITED STATES COMMISSIONER OF EDUCATION."[29]

The real issue now is not so much the problem of illegal diploma mills but rather the possibility that legitimate, accredited institutions will begin to look more and more like their fraudulent relatives. In other words, legit schools can easily begin catering to students as consumers or customers by supplying an education that is little more than prepackaged exams and reading material, if it is even that, administered by an underpaid contingent workforce, itself often dependent on so-called customer satisfaction for its continued employment. So an institution may be entirely legitimate, but the education it provides in an effort to compete in the e-learning marketplace can look more and more like the degraded training and the meaningless degrees provided by the fraudulent diploma mill. Ultimately, it is fraud, perhaps not in the strict legal definition, but students are certainly getting cheated out of a quality education.

Distance education has, for most if not all of its history, not only represented great educational potential but also given rise to fundamental questions of academic integrity, commitment to students, and accountability. Noble, in *Digital Diploma Mills*, notes that "by 1926 there were over three hundred [for-profit correspondence schools] in the United States."[30] A considerable sales force, generally working on commission, along with direct mail campaigns and print advertising, generated enrollment. What mattered, ultimately, was creating demand for correspondence courses and degrees, in large measure by peddling the flexibility, and sometimes the ease, with which such courses and degrees could be completed relative to their traditional classroom counterparts. The fundamental for-profit nature of the scheme left true learning low on the list of priorities. Indeed, Noffsinger reported in his 1926 study that, according to a survey of 75 correspondence schools, a scant 2.6 percent of students completed the courses in which they had enrolled. This makes completion rates in modern distance learning situations look pretty good.

Again, though, the point is not to denigrate online universities or for-profit institutions like the University of Northern Washington. In many cases, these businesses are marketing themselves explicitly and specifically to working adults who need maximum efficiency from their educational experience. So a campus—if one exists at all—is likely to be located near an interstate off-ramp and will afford generous parking for its commuting student body. And students may have no interest in the social extras found on traditional campuses, like student commons areas, athletic or dining facilities, or a campus bookstore. Some schools, like the University of Phoenix, are up front about offering job-specific training and contend that the vast majority of their student body has already completed the general education that more traditional schools provide. These education businesses often serve an entirely legitimate educational niche, and their students may be, on the whole, completely satisfied.

But what we are seeing more and more often, and more and more obviously, is that the kind of market-logic evidenced by for-profit, highly niche-market educational corporations is filtering widely into all kinds of institutions. This represents a looming and potentially serious crisis in higher education. As many commentators observe, the trend we would prefer to see is one toward greater emphasis on what are often called general education ideals—critical and creative thinking, exposure to and appreciation for diverse cultures and world views, and expanded horizons. The narrow and instrumental training that is often the hallmark of for-profit education and that is too much becoming evident in higher education generally does little to prepare students for what organizations like the American Association of Colleges and Universities describe as "the real-world demands of work, citizenship, and life in a complex and fast-changing society."[31]

Evidence of a degraded curriculum or of education dominated by a business model can often be discovered outside specific teaching situations. For example, Noble writes of the conditions surrounding early correspondence school efforts to generate enrollment. This task often fell specifically to salespeople: "the sales forces were encouraged to sign up any and all prospects, however ill-prepared for the coursework, in order to fulfill their quotas and reap their commissions."[32] We perhaps find the modern equivalent in such oddly titled positions as this one, advertised by one online university: "Enrollment Counselor/ Account Executive." The position announcement, on Careerbuilder. com, reveals the underlying tensions of for-profit education.[33] The rhetoric of a higher calling abounds: the position appeals to those who "recognize the value of higher education" and who "wish to help others achieve their educational goals." The job ad continues: "This career is professionally and personally rewarding as you help others achieve a better future through education." In addition to a "passion for education," however, "sales experience entailing one-on-one interaction is preferred." The position requires a "proven sales record." And, in case we forgot, "customer service, sales or marketing experience entailing one-on-one interaction" and "inside and/or outside sales experience" are both a plus.

One fears that the corporate focus here might be on drop money, a phrase that comes to us from the earliest days of correspondence education. It refers to student tuition collected without much regard for whether that particular student is likely to succeed. Noffsinger, in *Correspondence Schools*, levels a serious charge against many of the early correspondence schools: "more and more the promoter of correspondence schools tends to be of the type that knows nothing and cares less for educational standards. He sees only the possibility of reaping a rich harvest from dupes through clever advertisements and shrewd campaigns."[34] Of the salesman whose task it was to generate enrollment (the Enrollment Counselor/Account Executives of their day), Noffsinger writes, "Salesmen are usually paid commissions on the number of enrollments they obtain. This...is a dangerous practice. It leads to the enrollment of many students in no way qualified to take a course by their previous preparation or experience."[35]

In perhaps too many cases, lax (or absent) gatekeeping efforts on the part of institutions, public and for-profits alike, which should otherwise be in place to ensure that only those students who are legitimately likely to succeed are allowed to enroll, resemble a little too closely the unethical operations of the correspondence school sales forces of old. This problem is magnified when it comes to online learning, since Internet delivery often means low cost on the part of the school/business but also, and primarily, because distance education means that the potential customer base can be widespread. If the modus operandi is profit (either explicitly or, more often, implicitly) and if the customer base is anybody with a computer and an Internet connection, the opportunity for lax enrollment standards is self-evident. Institutions may not commit fraud, necessarily, but allowing students with a modem-based Internet connection to enroll in online courses is outright unethical in all but the fewest cases.

The absence of efforts to improve overall success rates prior to enrollment—which may, of course, decrease online enrollment by limiting it to those with basic technical skills and hardware components in place—is part of what continues to contribute to the general cultural view of online education as inferior to its traditional, face-to-face counterpart. For example, a Zogby poll of more than 5,000 adults, conducted in 2007, found that only 27 percent of respondents agreed that "online universities and colleges provide the same quality of education as traditional institutions." Those polled also imagined that employers and academic professionals perceived the quality of online education to be quite poor, though survey evidence actually suggests that chief academic officers often believe that online learning is on par with its traditional classroom counterpart. Clearly, though, while the perception of the quality of online learning has improved in recent years, especially as reported by those within academia itself, the cultural stigma attached to online learning remains.[36]

What has plagued distance education from its initial beginnings to its manifestation now as e-learning of all kinds has been the stigma of a dehumanized student-teacher relationship. In fact, Noffsinger, in *Correspondence Schools,* notes that a chief weakness of distance education was often "lack of personal contact between teacher and student."[37] Today, online learning is often understood (by students and by faculty) to be self-paced learning. In most cases, however, distance learning is ideally not entirely self-paced learning and does not simply involve each individual student working through material at his or her own pace. In fact, the most effective online learning invariably involves extensive asynchronous and synchronous engagement opportunities for students to interact with each other and with the professor via even simple applications like virtual chat or electronic discussion boards. In the entirely self-paced learning model, each student in a class— thought that term hardly applies—may be at entirely different points within a course.

For the public perception of online learning to improve—or for it to continue to improve—educators need to focus specifically on developing further synchronous, collaborative components in online courses. This invariably means, though, that distance learning will be less and less the flexible learning that it is so often conflated with today.

WHERE MIGHT THE HISTORY OF DISTANCE LEARNING GO?

Recent distance learning models may indicate where we are headed, at least in the near future. For example, an early but close relative of current online distance education is the telecourse. In this case, course content is offered via video tape or disc, CD ROM, or cable TV programming. The touted benefits of the telecourse model have always been that students need not be on campus regularly and that learning, in most cases, can be entirely self-paced. Opportunities for interaction between student and professor and among students themselves are clearly limited. Often, telecourse students are still required to be close enough to campus to check materials out of a library or learning resource center and take tests at a testing center. Alternately, they might have to be within the cable market for courses that are provided on cable TV. So, unlike online learning, the telecourse model does not represent a delivery mode for institutions that significantly increases their potential enrollment base. In terms of the technology of distance education, we have come a long way, though the push remains toward tapping into perceived student demand for even greater flexibility.

Educational content can now be delivered to personal, mobile broadband devices, like Apple's iPhone.[38] Although such educational offerings are not widespread, in November 2007, Cyber University of Japan—a private, for-profit institution—offered a course, "Mysteries of the Pyramids," which was delivered entirely via mobile phone. Sakuji Yoshimura, who runs the Pyramids course, asserts that "Our duty as educators is to respond to the needs of people who want to learn." The course could be accessed only via the SoftBank 3G phone, using the "S-Appli" function.[39] Cyber University is owned by the SoftBank Company, a major mobile carrier.[40]

As mobile phone technology improves (network connection speed, processing power, more sophisticated Web browsing and audio and video applications), delivery of online course content via cell phone may work almost identically to delivery of content through a desktop or laptop computer. One might argue that, at this point, mobile phones are more like very small personal computers than they are like traditional telephones.

However, if this is the direction that technology is taking us—toward greater and greater flexibility in course delivery—we must be careful not to lose those elements so fundamental to quality education, particularly as we move into the 21st century. Among the most basic aspects of real learning are collaboration and student interaction. In many ways, an entire college course delivered via cell phone seems predicated not on sound pedagogy but on the wish to respond to perceived market demand—educators giving students what they want—especially demand for flexible learning. We end up with little more than a high-tech telecourse. And it is ironic that entirely self-paced learning might actually be delivered through an advanced communications device.

Is it possible to respond to the demand for flexible learning, to take advantage of impressive advances in mobile technology, but to not lose sight of the pedagogical importance of collaboration and interaction? As we saw at the start of this chapter, perhaps hybridity again offers us a nonexclusive, best-of-both-worlds scenario. Imagine a course that requires students to meet face-to-face for part of the time but that also works via content delivered through an advanced cell phone, one capable of streaming video and audio, of displaying content in a readable format, and of allowing the user to communicate with classmates via discussion boards or to collaborate through Web 2.0 applications like a wiki.

The point, as we prepare to look at how hybrid classes are working now, is to think about where they might be going and exactly what forces—educational and market—will shape the future of distance and hybrid learning. Without input from educators themselves, whose interest is ideally in student success and not the bottom line, the future of online education is very likely to trend toward technology as a means purely to capture market share. If self-paced flexibility as an educational mode generates high profit at relatively low cost, then surely for-profit institutions will trend in that direction, to be followed, undoubtedly, by traditional not-for-profit institutions. Resistance to technology itself will not amount to anything. But informed resistance to technology in education as a means only to increase the profit margin is absolutely crucial.

CHAPTER 5

Hybrids in Action

In this chapter, we look at a series of blended learning examples. First, we examine snapshots of hybrid courses as they are currently being taught by a group of my colleagues at the College of DuPage. All of these educators are operating under the same contractual conditions and are working within the same institutional climate. We can also see, in this single-institution view, how challenges and successes in hybrid course design and delivery often bridge disciplinary lines. This reinforces the point that developing and delivering effective hybrid courses—advertising them effectively, supporting faculty effectively—takes institutional vision, even where the initial impetus for particular hybrid course design comes from particular faculty members. Successful and ongoing hybrid course development will not happen effectively if individual faculty are left to work alone with little or no broad support.

What we also find is that, while increasing blended offerings as an institutional mandate can provide the opportunity for faculty members to re-imagine curricula from the ground up in terms of advanced or cutting-edge technology, hybrid courses do not necessarily have to include complicated technology to be successful. In fact, many of the blended courses being taught by my colleagues are not especially technology intensive. Yet the courses themselves are, by all accounts, quite successful. In short, we find in this institutional snapshot evidence against one of the fundamental misapprehensions about blended learning: that to be successful, blended learning must involve complex technologies. This simply is not the case.

We also take a look in this chapter at an example of an effective hybrid program—a series of courses that includes both online and face-to-face components. Additionally, we examine the experience of a student in a hybrid program to find out, from her perspective, what works best in the blended model. To round out these various perspectives, we also look at a few examples of very different hybrids as they are being taught in colleges and universities across the United States. What we see is that, while some similarities emerge, even in widely divergent educational settings, the rule tends to be one of variation.

Before we get into the classroom, however, it is worth revisiting once again the terms we use to define blended learning and, more crucially, the way in which these courses need to be advertised on an institutional level to set the stage for student success. Even the best-designed hybrid class is unlikely to produce positive results if students are arriving the first day with no idea that they have enrolled in a blended course.

DEFINING TERMS (AGAIN) AND UPFRONT ADVERTISING

At the outset of this book, we looked at the shifting terminology surrounding blended/hybrid/mixed-mode/flexible/other models of course design and delivery. This state of pre-decision—a more positive and useful term than indecision—can be productive, as the multiple terms may connote different aspects of hybrid or blended learning. As such, they allow us to think quite broadly about this learning model's various educational precedents, including correspondence education, strictly online learning, and blended models like field and experiential studies. We also noted the various cultural associations attached to terms like "hybrid" as they circulate outside academe. The shifting terminology is further complicated, however, when we consider exactly how institutions define the learning model on a practical and contractual level.

For example, a hybrid course can be defined as a course in which students meet face-to-face at least 50 percent of the time. You would think that such a straightforward division of class time would be the norm, but this may not actually be the case. In fact, a common misconception among those who are not already teaching hybrids and among administrations that imagine hybrids as a straightforward means to address space and/or scheduling problems on campus is that the bulk of hybrids follow a simple 50/50 split. The related assumption is that the 50/50 split plays out as one day in the classroom and one day out each week. Many hybrids may be arranged this way, of course, but perhaps not as many as is commonly thought.

Some faculty may even be interested in experimenting with a number of different arrangements over the course of many semesters. Further, some definitions of hybrid classes require just 30 percent face-to-face time, with the remaining time accounted for online.[1] The immediate concern for likely student success is whether or not an institution has a mechanism in place to advertise to students not just that a class is a hybrid but exactly what this means on a course-by-course basis. A student might take two hybrid classes that are drastically different, for example: one might meet face-to-face 80 percent of the time (more akin to a traditional class), while another meets online 70 percent of the time (more akin to a strictly online class).

Related to issues of basic structural variability is the issue of technology. Perhaps because there is likely to be an online component in a hybrid class, blended learning is often presumed to involve cutting-edge technology. And, because the blended delivery mode is relatively new to the majority of faculty and students, there may even be the implication that the model is experimental in some sense and thus that the technology involved will be equally experimental.

The implications for both students and faculty that follow from the often incorrect equation of hybrid, technology, and complexity are considerable. A common assumption, but one that is not necessarily correct, is that students and faculty must be technologically inclined and savvy to be successful. This certainly presents a barrier for faculty if they perceive that teaching a hybrid class will necessitate a major investment of time and energy in technology self-education, since they imagine themselves having to use and troubleshoot a number of complicated online applications. Students may feel equally intimidated if they perceive hybrid classes to involve complicated technology.

We begin to see that a crucial part of successfully growing hybrid course offerings involves providing clarity about just what hybrid means and about just how technology actually figures into any particular course. Often, class schedule listings for hybrid courses include text like this: "HYBRID COURSE: 50% IN CLASS (WEDNESDAYS), 50% ONLINE...MUST BE FAMILIAR WITH AND HAVE ACCESS TO THE INTERNET."[2] This does not tell us much about exactly how technology plays a role in the class, though it does at least alert students to the fact that a portion of the class will occur online and that (of course) they must have online access. The brief description even identifies the percentage breakdown of online and f2f time, which can be enormously helpful for students to know as they select classes for a semester and before they arrive for class the first day.

The onus is on the individual faculty member to work with campus scheduling and/or with an immediate supervisor to ensure that as much information as possible about a particular class is made available to students. Efforts to provide students with access to fuller course descriptions would also certainly pay off in improved student success. Imagine, for example, that the course description cited was clickable in an online course schedule and the link took students to a paragraph description of the particular course, not just to a generic catalog description. This arrangement might take additional planning and coordination on the part of individual faculty and the offices responsible for producing the course schedule every term, but the investment would be worthwhile. Students who took time to read the course description would obviously have a much better sense of what their hybrid course was going to involve, and faculty might enjoy a student group that was aware of and enthusiastic about the chance to work with technology in a nontraditional teaching model that involved face-to-face and online time.

But try going to the online class schedules for a couple of different colleges and universities. Can you determine what courses are hybrid and exactly what that means operationally? In some cases, hybrid courses are not indicated as such in course schedules. The discovery that the class for which you have registered will meet online for half of the time must come as quite a surprise to some students on the first day. The situation is no picnic from the faculty perspective, either, since teachers face the challenge of selling the basic hybrid principle before even getting into the actual work for the class.

In other cases, hybrid courses are simply coded in the scheduling system as "Irregular" and are lumped together with any number of kinds of classes, like those that do not run for the standard term length. Clearly, the more that is done at all institutional levels to inform students about what they are in for, the better.

HYBRIDS ACROSS AN INSTITUTION

Ada Wainwright, Psychology

Professor Wainwright, who earned her Ph.D. at the University of Illinois, began teaching at the College of DuPage in Fall 2002. She teaches General Psychology and Developmental Psychology. Dr. Wainwright first began including technology in her classes by teaching Web-enhanced versions of her classroom courses. The term "Web-enhanced" indicates a class that includes some technology use—maybe content delivered through a course management system or an online discussion board—but does not trade face-to-face seat time for any of those online activities. Professor Wainwright also teaches fully online classes in addition to her traditional and hybrid courses. This puts her in a good position to evaluate the strengths and weaknesses of the various delivery modes.

Her move to hybrid teaching occurred largely at the invitation from her dean, who at one point encouraged faculty to develop hybrid and online versions of existing classes. The opportunities afforded by mixed-mode teaching for reaching a broad student audience resonated with Professor Wainwright's desire to design curricula that would be attractive to community college students, many of whom might be juggling multiple obligations in addition to school, including work and family.

Wainwright's hybrid psychology course provides an excellent example of what might be termed a relatively low-tech hybrid. That is, it does trade face-to-face seat time for online time, but the online activities are relatively straightforward and do not involve any applications outside Blackboard, the course management system used at the College of DuPage.[3]

And, while Dr. Wainwright remains interested in broadening her use of technology in her blended classes, she is conscious that with increasingly complex technology comes the problem of losing students who may be so worried about the technical demands of a course that they simply drop the class. This represents a tension that is likely to be felt by many, if not all, educators working in mixed-mode delivery. On the one hand, we would like to be using technology to its fullest in designing courses that afford students the opportunity to exercise a number of learning styles and to participate in collaborative knowledge building; however, as technology complexity increases, so does the likelihood that the very students we are trying to reach (that broadly diverse group with potentially very different learning styles) will be scared away. In short, efforts to increase accessibility can actually have the opposite effect.

Recall that it is not necessarily students' actual facility with technology that inevitably matters. As we have seen, students' perception of the technological demands of a particular course is pivotal. Many students are extremely comfortable when it comes to Facebook, MySpace, and other forms of social networking or communication. Surprisingly, at least for some teachers, this does not translate into students being receptive to learning other (even very similar) technology applications. Faculty who end up teaching hybrid classes soon realize the significant time that must be invested up front (and face-to-face) to get students comfortable with even the most basic digital applications.

It is worth noting that, while we may often hear that students are turned off a course because of its technology component, at least some students simply use the technology requirement as a convenient reason for not completing a class. It is not, in fact, the technological demands per se that turn students away. Technology just emerges in some cases as a convenient reason for withdrawing when, in fact, entirely other factors may be in play.

Professor Wainwright uses technology in her hybrid teaching primarily to assess regularly the degree to which her students are learning course content. She uses the Blackboard exam feature throughout her course to have students work out of class, taking weekly quizzes based on textbook reading. Notably, while the weekly quizzes are to be taken online, Professor Wainwright administers the midterm and final exams in the face-to-face classroom setting. Again, while she considers adding more dynamic technology to her hybrid classes, ideally to facilitate greater communication among students outside of their f2f meeting time, the tech component she currently has in place serves a specific purpose, responds to a clear course need, and presents very little technological difficulty even for the least tech-savvy of her students. A substantial benefit that Professor Wainwright derives from her hybrid design, she notes, is that it requires students to work online on a regular basis. This forms what Wainwright refers to as a mandatory attendance policy, though attendance just happens to be virtual.

It is not surprising to find that students with better attendance earn higher course grades. The 2007 Community College Survey of Student Engagement (CCSSE) reports that Paul D. Camp Community College—working logically from statistics that relate attendance to success—introduced an "attendance program for all gatekeeper courses" that involves giving weekly quizzes.[4] This seems to be common sense, and yet the 2007 CCSSE is also clear that the bulk ("close to two-thirds") of students at community colleges have significant obligations outside school. So attendance improves student results, yet the students most often in need of additional academic support are those who may already struggle to attend classes regularly. Something as simple as a weekly online quiz delivered flexibly, in a hybrid class, has obvious implications for making attendance much easier for students with considerable external demands on their time. The basic weekly online quiz within the hybrid format is a straightforward technology. But it has immediate and significant implications for improved student success.

The course schedule that Professor Wainwright supplies in her syllabus is also very clear about how face-to-face and online time is coordinated, in this case around content themes. Where this particular psychology course, in its nonhybrid format, would normally meet face-to-face twice per week, Professor Wainwright's hybrid course meets face-to-face only one day per week. Textbook readings and face-to-face learning are connected directly to an assessment mechanism: the weekly online quizzes. In this way, students are provided with an ongoing measure of their understanding of course material. Wainwright is also able to see whether or not students are successfully understanding course content.

Professor Wainwright's hybrid General Psychology class provides an excellent example of a hybrid format that does not involve a wide variety of technology applications. In fact, Professor Wainwright's straightforward use of technology responds to one of the most frequently identified reasons that students take entirely online classes: flexibility. The hybrid design in this case also reflects Professor Wainwright's sensitivity to the student population that she is generally serving, a population that benefits from the flexibility of online assessment tools. The face-to-face time afforded in the hybrid course still lets Wainwright establish a connection with her students, which, she notes, is extremely important. She can provide a sense of what she calls "embodied knowledge" that is much more difficult to provide in classes that take place entirely online.

In 2005, Professor Wainwright was part of a study at the College of DuPage that looked to assess student success in, and to collect student opinions about, hybrid courses. A group of 56 students—23 enrolled in General Psychology, 11 in Developmental Psychology: Childhood, and 22 in Introduction to Sociology—were asked to complete a survey about their experiences taking a hybrid class. Notably, 20 percent listed the convenience of the once-per-week face-to-face meeting as their primary motivation for taking the hybrid version of the class. This flexibility was the most common reason for opting for the hybrid model.

Survey data also revealed that students who enrolled in a traditional classroom class and who worked increased hours at a job outside school fared worse than those who worked fewer hours at an outside job. This did not hold true for students enrolled in the hybrid course, as they seemed to be able to manage the extra hours working a job, thanks likely to the more flexible learning provided by the hybrid mode. This finding is particularly significant for those at community colleges, since such an institution is relatively more likely to attract students with considerable work demands in addition to their scholastic obligations.

The final results of the survey indicate no significant differences in performance between traditional classroom and hybrid sections of the same course. In fact, so many variables affect student performance that it would be difficult to determine whether delivery mode alone was responsible for statistically significant differences in student performance for this relatively small sample size. So, while we do not find that the hybrid delivery mode necessarily improved student performance by any great measure, we do—more positively—find that the hybrid mode did not adversely affect student performance. And, beyond simple grade performance, students rated the quality of the hybrid courses they had completed as 4.50 on a 5-point scale. This postcourse survey asked students about such elements as course organization and grading methods and about whether they would recommend a hybrid course to a friend, which many said they would.

As we have seen earlier, when it comes to entirely online classes, it is no surprise that student success is tied to reliable access to a computer and an Internet connection at home (not just at work, school, or a public library). Professor Wainwright's survey provides equally interesting insights into variables that most significantly affect student success in introductory psychology classes. Particularly crucial for success in the hybrid format is—again not surprisingly—availability of a home computer. To most, this probably confirms what common sense already tells us, though, when we look at how institutionally, hybrid classes are advertised and how they are supported, we often find that students are not actually required to have reliable home access to a computer and a high-speed Internet connection.

This is precisely the tension that many schools face when it comes to online delivery modes: the institutional desire to grow online and hybrid offerings meets the pedagogical imperative to position students for success. One wonders what would happen to online and hybrid course enrollments, for example, if class schedule listings made it clear that students were required to have high-speed Internet access at home.

Professor Wainwright has more recently talked about deepening the types of technology she uses in her classes to include more collaborative and discussion-based applications. And Dr. Wainwright's experience quite likely is similar to that of many faculty members. She was interested in teaching with technology and had exposure to technology-assisted learning as a graduate student. She then continued to explore it as a faculty member, benefiting particularly from an administrator who encouraged faculty to innovate if it made sense for them to do so. Wainwright's first attempts at hybridizing a course reflected an approach to technology that put primacy on meeting a known student demand (flexibility) and on accomplishing course objectives more efficiently (online quizzes to track learning).

Professor Wainwright now finds herself interested in exploring more intricate uses of technology. This inevitably means that the technical side of her hybrid courses will become more involved, first for her and then for her students. Undoubtedly, then, students will have to have reliable home access to the Internet, and both professor and students will need to be supported by the institution as a whole.

The trajectory of Professor Wainwright's experience ultimately provides a useful example, since it is one that many faculty may experience. Her experience may suggest what many hybrid courses will look like at institutions that are urging more and more faculty to consider teaching in the blended mode. If significant numbers of faculty begin teaching blended classes at more or less the same time, then campuses may experience an initial period (lasting a few semesters, perhaps) of courses that use basic features of course management systems but not much more. Demands for IT support and for basic technical requirements like bandwidth or online storage space could be fairly light. However, following this first iteration of hybrid courses as they are being made available on a broad basis, institutions may very well see a large number of faculty who become interested in using much more complicated and varied digital tools. In other words, demand for institutional resources and support—including faculty development opportunities and hardware and software improvements—may become much more intensive after an initial period of hybrid course development and teaching.

Naheed Hasan, Psychology

Dr. Naheed Hasan has been teaching at the College of DuPage since 2002. She is a colleague of Dr. Wainwright's, and she too teaches a hybrid version of Introduction to Psychology. Additionally, Hasan teaches Child Development in both traditional and hybrid versions.

Dr. Hasan, like Dr. Wainwright, initially became interested in hybrids early in her career at the college, and, like Dr. Wainwright, she became interested in hybrids when her supervising dean called on faculty to increase the number of blended versions of the department's core courses. Dr. Hasan saw this kind of curricular development as a good opportunity to distinguish herself as a junior faculty member helping to foster a new initiative. The administrative desire to broaden Psychology offerings at the college dovetailed nicely with Hasan's interest in increasing the flexibility of her own schedule.

This marks what might be a fairly common confluence of pressures that lead faculty to explore alternative delivery and mixed mode teaching. There are real administrative pressures to diversify and deepen course offerings—and these kinds of pressures may be felt particularly by newly hired faculty members. Many new faculty are also facing an extremely heavy teaching load, and some may be, like the students they are educating, balancing a number of family obligations as they begin their careers. The opportunity for a less rigid classroom schedule that hybrid courses can represent often has a very real practical appeal. In other words—and this is the crucial point—we may find that the move to hybrid teaching is not motivated primarily by a desire on the part of faculty members to include more technology (or to include technology more often) in course design and delivery. This does not mean that pedagogical concerns do not ultimately prevail in faculty members' interest in, or move toward, teaching hybrid classes. Nor should we understand a more flexible schedule as resulting in less work. In fact, the opposite is almost always true. But we see that technology, potentially the most visible defining feature of the blended environment, may actually have little to do with faculty motivation to explore the teaching mode in the first place.

The practical implications of scheduling and flexibility that can motivate faculty toward mixed teaching are particularly relevant, though, as we consider 21st-century learning objectives that are calling for greater and greater elements of student collaboration and real-time discussion. When, or if, online and hybrid learning become more and more synchronous, we will necessarily be cutting into the flexibility of the online and blended modes. As was noted earlier, this could easily affect otherwise booming enrollment in alternative delivery formats.

But we may also see fewer faculty interested in pursuing hybrid teaching if it does not afford the flexibility that strictly asynchronous online learning does. Professor Hasan makes the point quite clearly, though, that while her hybrid Introduction to Psychology does offer greater flexibility (for both herself and her students), it consumes much more of her time than does her traditional Introduction to Psychology class.

The online and face-to-face time in Professor Hasan's hybrid Introduction to Psychology is divided more or less evenly, though not exactly in a 50/50 split, favoring slightly more f2f time. In-class and online activities remain closely coordinated, however. Hasan uses applications in Blackboard to have her students respond each week to short answer and essay questions. Classroom time involves the presentation (by Hasan) and exploration (as a group) of complex concepts. Time is also available for in-class group work that focuses on applying material that students have read outside class and have already reflected on in assignments available through Blackboard. Face-to-face meetings also provide opportunities for student presentations, which forces students to consider their paralinguistic behaviors in ways that strictly text-based online communication does not.

In its basic division of online and face-to-face activities, Professor Hasan's hybrid course provides a good example of how each learning mode can be exploited to tap its strengths: the online component is ideal for allowing students to work through information and to craft written responses at their own pace, in a concentrated and reflective way, while the face-to-face environment is best suited for the embodied experience of discussion and presentation.

While Professor Hasan may have immediately derived attractive practical or nontechnological benefits from designing and teaching hybrid courses, she has taken great care to construct a pedagogically sound course that adheres to all of the guidelines and learning objectives for Introduction to Psychology as they are laid out by her department. In fact, having taught and revised her hybrid courses over the past few years, Hasan now notes that students who take the hybrid version of her Introduction to Psychology course may actually be getting a more enriched experience than similarly motivated students who opt for the traditional classroom mode. Students in hybrid sections are responsible for covering the assigned reading each week so that they can complete the online discussion and response questions. This marks an ideal aspect of the hybrid mode in that we see how basic technology (offered entirely through a course management system) makes possible consistent student assessment. This kind of assessment is much more cumbersome and constrained when a class is always meeting face-to-face, and is often possible only when assessment is reduced to multiple-choice quizzes, since these do not require the time for reflection and consideration that written responses might. As a result, because students are being asked to respond in writing to essay and discussion questions every week, they must formulate thoughts and synthesize ideas into communicable form. Hasan notes that the quality of the classroom time actually improves when students are regularly challenged to read and respond in writing to course content outside of the classroom.

Regarding student retention and success, Dr. Hasan's situation is likely typical. In the hybrid class, student retention is lower than in the comparable traditional course section, yet student success is higher. Problems of lower retention are quite often the result of conditions that are external to the course itself or to any of its technical components per se. Hasan notes, for example, that a number of students consistently show up for her hybrid section the first day assuming that, since the class meets only once per week, it will require only half the work.

Despite a class schedule, published each semester and available online, that provides students with information about delivery mode, be it hybrid or online, students still arrive to the course mis- (or un-)

informed. Hasan estimates that anywhere between 25 percent and 30 percent of students arrive at her hybrid course on the first day not understanding what the hybrid model actually entails. The result, statistically at least, is lower retention.

However, just as many students are, in Professor Hasan's experience, actively selecting the hybrid model because they do understand the implications of the format. This generally means that students who register and complete the hybrid course achieve higher grades than do students in the traditional classroom model. Informal feedback further suggests that a number of students who complete a hybrid course successfully are interested in taking more of the same.

Professor Hasan takes great care in making students comfortable with the technology involved, spending extra time outside class with students who are not immediately comfortable with even basic computer-based applications, not to mention the intensive first-day overview and f2f step-by-step instruction she offers.

Although student retention may be lower in Dr. Hasan's hybrid Introduction to Psychology than in her traditional classroom course, student success is often better. The hybrid version of the course offers many more opportunities for students with different learning styles to engage the material. Further, as we have seen for students in Professor Wainwright's hybrid psychology classes, Dr. Hasan's students are required to read the textbook and to formulate weekly written responses based on class concepts as part of their online work. Some students are able to participate in the class in a much more engaged and meaningful way than might be the case when participation is limited to face-to-face, classroom discussion.

An irony that Hasan—among many faculty that teach blended classes—has observed is that, while distance or computer-based learning may seem cold and impersonal (this is the stereotype, at any rate), many students may actually be more engaged in what is going on than they would be in a classroom. It is possible to daydream in a physical classroom environment, in which participation is not necessarily required. But students cannot so easily disengage online, since each and every student must contribute thoughts and ideas. Basic course management technology allows faculty to see who has responded to a discussion board prompt and who has not. Faculty can even track who has logged in to a course and who has not. In a physical classroom discussion, participation by half the class is sometimes counted a success. That might mean that 17 students out of some 35 have contributed their ideas. Move this to an online discussion board as a required assignment in a blended class and you can easily see all 35 students adding to the virtual discussion. The computer-mediated situation thus can produce greater student engagement than might the physical classroom situation, even though conventional wisdom often imagines the reverse.

Professor Hasan reports that her experience with designing and teaching hybrid classes has been overall positive, and she often sees better learning results for students who persist in the hybrid class than she finds in those students who complete her traditional classroom course. However, like Professor Wainwright, Hasan finds herself at a point that is familiar to many faculty members who teach hybrids: she would like to further enhance the technology component in her class, including more complex, focused group discussion opportunities for students, for example. Yet she has already invested considerable time in the intense (and ongoing) self-education that is required for those wishing to introduce technology into their curricula.

In many cases, the rhetoric of continual improvement and excellence that is publicly appealing for many institutions is not matched with support for faculty who have already undertaken major curricular innovation and redesign. A simple course-release policy could provide faculty with the time to truly redesign a hybrid class. In this scenario, a faculty member's teaching load might be reduced by one class for a semester. However, this kind of so-called inefficient use of faculty work time is so far off the radar for some institutions that it may appear laughable. It is exactly the kind of investment that institutions need to make to support effective blended learning, though.

Finally, Professor Hasan's situation is instructive in that the higher student success but lower student retention rates she sees in her hybrid courses relative to the traditional classroom courses encapsulate in a focused way the very broad potentials and challenges of hybrid teaching. In Professor Hasan's Introduction to Psychology class, we really do see the best of what face-to-face learning and online learning can provide. Yet institutional efforts to educate students about just what it means to take a hybrid class and what the demands (technical and temporal) will be are not yet refined enough to prevent a third of those students from walking into the classroom on the first with little clue as to what they have signed up for.

Mitchell Fisher, Economics

Mitch Fisher holds an M.B.A. from the University of Michigan and an M.S. from the University of Illinois at Urbana-Champaign. He began teaching at the College of DuPage in 2002 and very early in his career—2003–2004—began designing and teaching hybrid economics classes, including courses on microeconomics and macroeconomics.

He divides hybrid course time evenly between face-to-face and online activities, meeting once per week for an entire class period face-to-face, whereas the traditional classroom section would meet twice per week. The online time allows students to review lecture notes, work on practice problems, and complete other self-assessments, all provided within the Blackboard course management system. Additional Web research is often required as part these online assignments.

The online component of Professor Fisher's hybrid classes is relatively low-tech. But the technology serves to achieve important pedagogical goals and remains closely integrated with face-to-face classroom work. The straightforward technology component also means that Professor Fisher sees very few technology-related problems that might discourage his students. Further, as we have seen in previous examples, Professor Fisher has designed the online component of his economics hybrid to provide students with opportunities for weekly self-assessment. While some extra practice, which prepares students for in-class exams, is not graded, students do receive feedback and can repeat problems.

Professor Fisher's hybrids provide another good example of course design that reflects the basic principle of the medium serving the pedagogical ends to which it is best suited. Face-to-face classroom time proves ideal for dynamic, large-group interaction and for the presentation of complex concepts. In this setting, students have the opportunity to ask questions and receive immediate clarification. Online time, which lets students work at a more flexible pace, is ideal for frequent, regularly occurring self-assessment, especially in cases where students are able to analyze mistakes and repeat problems until they are successful.

Professor Fisher has students take exams during their f2f class meetings, since it is much easier for him to control testing in the classroom environment. He also has students submit written projects in hard copy, which is easier for him to grade and to return to students, and which removes any potential e-mail or attachment problems students might run into. In other words, Professor Fisher has been careful to think about exactly what technology can make better for him and where it might simply introduce complications or issues.

Professor Fisher suggests that he is interested in incorporating more collaborative online opportunities or asynchronous discussions, though his hybrids are currently working well, meeting his pedagogical goals, and serving students. So, while the impulse to innovate might be present, he believes that significant changes can do more harm than good. As he notes, the adage "if it ain't broke, don't fix it" may well apply.

To consider this in a much broader context, clear institutional goals are paramount when it comes to learning and technology. And these institutional goals should not just be administrative goals. They are ideally crafted by constituent stakeholders, with representation from faculty (both full and part time), administration, and student support staff. Is technology in the classroom meant to represent a cutting-edge vision? Is being at the forefront of technology use in education important institutionally? Is rhetoric about technology and/as innovation declared publicly? Or is technology a secondary consideration to an effective pedagogy, which just happens to be enabled by certain online applications? Institutional missions, visions, and the public rhetoric that inevitably circulates about a school should ideally align with what is actually happening in classrooms.

For Professor Fisher specifically, there is, of course, the further investment of time and energy that it would take on his part to learn new online applications and to integrate them into his curricula effectively. Such demands on faculty energy, especially after the initial investment it usually takes to get a hybrid up and running in the first place, are daunting. Recall that many faculty members may have little to no technical expertise beyond basic Web skills (and often no specific training in online or hybrid course design) when they first enter the blended learning environment. Their move into blended learning can be motivated as much by professional, personal, or institutional pressures as by a core desire to use technology. Professor Fisher admits to mostly "learning on my own" when he first began developing his micro- and macroeconomics hybrids, for example.

The results, in Professor Fisher's experience, have been mostly positive. Student retention is not noticeably different in his hybrid sections from the retention rate in the traditional classroom offerings, though hybrid and classroom retention numbers are much better than for the online micro-and macro-courses (speaking perhaps to the major benefit of preserving some face-to-face contact between professor and student). Student success in classroom sections and in hybrid sections is also more or less the same. Grades may be slightly higher in hybrid sections, though this could as easily be a result of the time of day that the course is offered—late afternoon—which appeals to adult students more than to traditional college-age students. The adult group is often more motivated and focused on success at school, composed as it is of adults who may, at one time, have been traditional college-age students who were not so attentive to their studies. And students do benefit from the greater flexibility afforded by the hybrid mode. There still remains, though, a small percentage of students who arrive to class on the first day not understanding what a hybrid class involves or assuming that a class that meets half the time will involve half the work.

Lois Stanciak, Education

Professor Lois Stanciak has been teaching a hybrid Introduction to Education class since 2006. She holds an M.A. from the University of Chicago and an Ed.D. from Vanderbilt University and has been teaching at the College of DuPage since 2002. She further has extensive experience working in secondary educational settings, having been an associate and an assistant principal, as well as a director of student services and special education and gifted coordinator. Professor Stanciak, now as an education professor, has considerable knowledge of and investment in effective and innovative teaching strategies that work practically for a broad range of students. She is, in many cases, responsible for educating the educators of tomorrow.

As such, her move into hybrid teaching was motivated partly by her awareness of her audience—typically traditional-age college students—and the degree to which technology was playing a part in their lives. Stanciak also believes that she is modeling the kind of curricular innovation that will be expected of many of her students in their future profession as teachers. In "Curricula Designed to Meet 21st Century Expectations," authors Alma R. Clayton-Pedersen and Nancy O'Neill observe that "Students' personal experience with technology is typically broad and in many cases very deep."[5] This seemed particularly true of the students that Professor Stanciak was routinely seeing in her Introduction to Education classes.

We also know that more and more K-12 educators are being tasked with curricular innovation, which often hinges on the use of technology in the classroom. Such innovation is, of course, much more effective if the teacher him- or herself has had previous exposure to classes in which technology has figured as a key component. Clayton-Pedersen and O'Neill also note that "Faculty's understanding of the teaching and learning power of technology needs to be increased" if curricular innovation is to be effective.[6] This assertion has proven to be doubly meaningful for Stanciak, who uses technology to re-envision her teaching and who is responsible for introducing potential future faculty members to the possibilities of technology in the classroom.

Professor Stanciak's Introduction to Education course is similar to the examples discussed earlier in that it divides course time equally between online and face-to-face modes. Since the class meets only once per week, however, the face-to-face meeting time itself is shortened, though students do in fact meet face-to-face every week (as would be the case for the nonhybrid course). This arrangement makes much more sense than if course time were to be divided so that students would meet face-to-face for an entire once-per-week period but then not again for another two weeks (i.e., no class meeting would occur the following week). A long gap between f2f meetings could easily prove problematic for ongoing student engagement.

As we have seen in earlier examples, the technology component in Professor Stanciak's class is relatively straightforward and is administered almost entirely through the Blackboard course management system. Students may be required to watch presentations online, visit and review education-related Web sites, take quizzes, and/or watch streaming video (this last is an ideal way for students to see other teachers in action).

Interestingly, while Professor Wainwright's hybrid psychology course uses the online component largely to measure whether students are learning classroom material that has been previously presented, often the online component in Professor Stanciak's class works to prepare students for an upcoming class meeting in which they might work in collaborative groups or discuss and apply concepts they have already encountered in their work online. This distinction in how the online and face-to-face components of a course can interact provides just a limited sense of the diversity of ways in which blended courses can be organized and exactly how face-to-face and online time can be related.

Professor Stanciak indicates that the benefits of teaching in the mixed mode include the opportunity to appeal to a number of different learning styles. Hands-on learning, for example, is particularly important for her education classes, though it would be difficult to duplicate in an entirely online, solely text-based, setting.[7] Students' accountability for their own learning is of equal importance. The hybrid format allows for the face-to-face time necessary for hands-on learning, while the online time remains ideal for students working through material and completing assessments on their own, providing them (and the professor) with feedback along with the time to reflect on material—pausing slide presentations or video streams, for example—which is not possible in the face-to-face format. Professor Stanciak took a number of online courses herself in order to understand the student perspective and to help her better design her hybrid course.

She, like many faculty members who are teaching hybrid courses, is also particularly open to continuing her own education—formally and informally—when it comes to online applications and their practicality for her class. She stresses the need for continual in-house professional development opportunities, including short workshops, extended faculty classes, and other face-to-face and online opportunities to help for busy faculty to learn about new online applications and new features in the course management system. It would make sense, Stanciak observes, to provide these kinds of opportunities online when feasible, given that the subject matter is effective use of technology for teaching. Practical how-tos might usefully be recorded and then collected in an online resource, for example, that interested faculty could download and view at their own pace.

Institutional efforts to offer these kinds of faculty development opportunities are crucial to fostering—and, importantly, for continually improving—technological innovation in the classroom. Making recorded professional development presentations available for later viewing, perhaps even catalogued through the campus library system, for example, is a logical step.

Professor Stanciak has received positive feedback from students who have taken her hybrid education course. Part of students' positive feedback stems from the fact that the online and face-to-face components of the hybrid are clearly related and are designed to complement each other. Students have the sense that they are, indeed, taking just one class and not two separate classes, one online and the other in the classroom. However, Stanciak reports that retention in the hybrid Introduction to Education is a problem. Generally, more students drop the hybrid course than from its traditional classroom counterpart.

The lower retention rate in the hybrid Introduction to Education is particularly surprising, because it is an elective course, attracting primarily (though not exclusively) those who have chosen education as a career field. And, while it is always difficult to determine with precision exactly why students do not persist through a course, Stanciak suggests that many students may be intimidated by the technological component of the course, despite its being relatively straightforward and although Professor Stanciak takes time during face-to-face meetings to introduce students to the technology involved and walks them through the basics.

Stanciak is now at the point where she would actually like to be adding more dynamic online applications to her course, such as virtual classrooms for multiparty, synchronous lecture and discussion. What might this do to retention, though? And to what extent would Professor Stanciak herself have to take on the role of IT specialist, not only walking students through basic online applications during the face-to-face component of the class but also diagnosing and addressing technical problems that students might be having? At some point, one begins to worry that the face-to-face time of a hybrid course will become overwhelmingly an exercise in prepping and troubleshooting for the online time.

As we noted previously, though, technology may only appear to be the culprit when it comes to lower than expected student retention and success. Technology stands out as an obvious difference between the elements of a hybrid and a traditional class and so may seem to be the sole cause of variances in student success or persistence between classes delivered in the two modes. However, the reasons behind such differences are almost always more nuanced. Technology might simply provide a convenient reason for students to withdraw when they are not particularly motivated to begin with. In the absence of an obvious scapegoat for withdrawing in the traditional classroom, some students perhaps persist though with less than stellar results.

In the case of Professor Stanciak's Introduction to Education course, offering time seems to play a key role relative to success and retention. The hybrid is usually offered at 1 P.M. in the afternoon. Because the course tends to attract primarily traditional-age college students and because those students generally choose morning classes over after-noon ones, the hybrid section of Introduction to Education tends to fill last, after all the other morning sections have filled. The hybrid course may end up populated with students for whom the early-afternoon time slot is not a first choice and whose schedules are not arranged for success. A further complicating factor is that students who do opt for the hybrid delivery mode are often surprised, according to Stanciak, that the 15 hours of observation, which require students to visit and observe actual teaching situations, are still required. The blended de-livery mode does not shortchange on those 15 hours. Some students, seeing the mixed-mode option in the college's course schedule, may assume that the observation hours will be accounted for differently or perhaps not at all. When students arrive to Professor Stanciak's hybrid course to discover that the observation hours are required, a few stu-dents simply drop the course.

And, as we have already noted, some students—a shrinking percent-age, one hopes, but a percentage nonetheless—inevitably arrive to the first class meeting of hybrid courses without understand the implica-tions of the hybrid format. Still others do understand what the hybrid course structure entails but do not factor in their own learning styles when opting for the mixed-mode class. In the course evaluation for one of Professor Stanciak's hybrid sections, for example, one student noted that "more class time" would have increased her understanding of the course material.

Perhaps this student discovered her ideal learning style during the hybrid class, but it is more likely that the student simply did not consider her learning style when considering the class delivery mode. It is sur-prising that a student who (apparently) learns better in the face-to-face environment would opt for a delivery mode involving only half of that delivery mode. Another student writes, "[I] wish I took a longer class so that we could discuss more." One wonders if more online discussion might have satisfied this student, though, again, the decision by a student looking for more classroom discussion to opt for a hybrid mode class is, from the faculty perspective at least, baffling. At least one of Professor Stanciak's students recognized the importance of aligning learning style with deliver mode for him- or herself, writing that "I would have liked more class time to get more in depth, but that's my fault for taking a hybrid class."

More common remains this kind of oddly positive sentiment: "I actually find a class I really enjoy and it only met [once] a week!" A fuller and more revealing context is represented in this student's comment: "I work two jobs, one full-time, one part-time because I'm guardian of my 3 younger siblings—can't afford internet and I worked while library was open." Clearly the flexibility of the hybrid mode was crucial for this student, but not having any home access to the Internet must have presented a serious challenge.

Professor Stanciak reports that learning outcomes look positive in the hybrid mode, despite the slightly higher withdrawal rate relative to that for the traditional delivery mode (the majority of the withdrawals coming very early in the course). Aside from some student feedback that reflects how unclear certain students are about their preferred learning style and/or the nature of a hybrid course, student response overall has been positive. For example, in almost all of the anonymous, qualitative surveys that Professor Stanciak has her students complete, class members indicate (often exuberantly) that they have a better understanding of the field of education. And certainly many students do understand what it means to take a hybrid class. One writes, for example, "online/hybrid idea works for people with flexible schedules."

Professor Stanciak's class—a good model of a hybrid course in and of itself—is also an excellent case of curricular innovation that provides students, themselves perhaps future educators, with an example of the kinds of technological demands that they are likely to face in their professional lives. Stanciak has benefited from her efforts to imagine her course differently, and she is modeling curricular innovation as a key component of the work of an educator.

A HYBRID PROGRAM

Master of Education in Educational Studies, University of Alberta

Unlike the previous examples, which suggest how individual courses might look in hybrid form, the graduate degree in Educational Studies,

offered as one of the University of Alberta's alternative delivery programs, gives us a look at how an entire program might be structured
on the hybrid learning model. The M.E.S. program affords us a look
at how hybrid learning is being used by a major research institution
at the graduate level. What we will see, though, is that while the details and contexts of this and the previous blended learning examples
might be quite different, the underlying premises for employing distance learning in combination with face-to-face interaction to produce
positive learning results are quite similar. An important element, related to blended learning, also in evidence in the M.E.S. example is the
effectiveness of cohort-based learning in enabling student success.[8]

The M.E.S. program is expressly designed for "working professionals who wish to complete a master's degree without taking time off
from work."[9] The target audience for the program is working teachers,
K-12. The program Web site indicates, for example, that "You can finish
the program in two years without taking a leave from your teaching
career." And, further, "Course assignments will be constructed around
a typical school year calendar."[10] The program features face-to-face
learning during two summer terms. These consist of three-week, full-
time residencies in years one and two of the program. The remainder
of the M.E.S. program occurs online during the fall and winter terms.
Structurally, the entire program is based on the hybrid model, rather
than each individual class being composed of both face-to-face and
online delivery modes.

Students move through the program as a cohort, usually of about
30 students. Natasja Larson, the program administrator, reports that
cohorts have been as large as 62, although that large number proved to
be challenging. In cases of high enrollment numbers, multiple smaller
cohorts are likely to be created.[11]

Use of the cohort model is in keeping with new directions in distance
education generally. As Larson indicates, "what helps our students
graduate is them supporting each other." This sense of an educational
community as part of distance learning marks an interesting move
away from conventional notions of distance education as a primarily individual, even self-paced, enterprise. A 2004 study that focused
on working K-12 educators who were taking graduate-level education
courses suggests that, for the sample under consideration, "blended
courses produce a stronger sense of community among students than
either traditional or fully online courses."[12]

Cohort-based learning may at first glance seem a counterintuitive
model to employ in the distance learning environment, but that is
only if we understand modern Web-based online learning as adhering
to the principles that have guided distance education historically as
purely correspondence learning. And, while Internet-based distance

education has certainly grown at least partially out of a long history of correspondence education, it affords such radically different opportunities for interaction between student and teacher, and among students themselves, that at some point we must re-imagine online learning as distinct from its correspondence school antecedent.

The Distance Education and Training Council (DETC) is a national accrediting agency for distance learning programs, including Web-based but also correspondence and self-paced programs. As we noted earlier, its accrediting standards and criteria were initially developed with the correspondence education model in mind. However, several DETC-accredited schools are turning from true self-paced correspondence education to online learning, and many of these schools are using the cohort model. In other words, many schools—even those that have traditionally provided self-paced courses via the mail—are introducing cohort learning as part of online distance education, rather than simply putting correspondence materials onto the Web and (as before) allowing students to work through the material at their own pace. This choice marks a significant direction in online education as it clearly favors educational quality and the student learning experience over technical ease. That is, it would be much simpler and cheaper to create an online degree program by putting existing correspondence materials on a Web site for individual students to access rather than designing, from the ground up, an entirely different framework for distance learning.

A U.S. Department of Education report on distance learning accreditation notes that many DETC-accredited schools are opting for the cohort model to allow for "greater interaction among students." And, further, "success rates are higher in a cohort-based model than in a self-paced model."[13] The University of Alberta's M.E.S. program does not happen to be accredited by the DETC, but it nevertheless provides an excellent example of how a distance education program can be effectively anchored in cohort learning.

Also, as is often the case, hybrid programs like the M.E.S. degree can develop as a response to very specific market needs. Programs can be tailored to a relatively narrow student niche, especially in the situation where entire degree programs are based on the flexibility afforded by distance education. Larson writes that the program:

was created to fill a significant and growing gap between supply and demand in continuing formal education for educators. That Alberta teachers and administrators and their districts were willing to invest up to $25,000 per head to have students complete graduate degrees from American universities made it clear that ongoing educational needs of K-12 educators were not being fully met by traditional graduate degree programs being offered by Alberta's three universities.[14]

In this case, the M.E.S. degree is targeted to working teachers who have summers off (thus the intensive face-to-face summer residencies) but who are teaching from September to June (during which time program courses are taken online).

The double-edged sword of flexibility presents itself yet again: the program targets working teachers, and program advertising promises a graduate degree in two years without the need to take time off work. So the marketing hook is clearly flexibility. Does this connote ease, however? How have M.E.S. program developers and faculty taken care to realize flexibility without compromising program rigor? Effective time management—upon which student success and retention so clearly depend—is highlighted as crucial. The program Web site also makes explicit that "students with good support and time management skills will find the program more rewarding." Furthermore, the application process involves completing a "Technology Compliance Checklist."[15]

Larson reports that a significant portion of the program's target audience is educators in rural or remote areas "who do not have access to face-to-face courses." Further considerations are made to include those educators whose "contractual obligations [make] full-time study sabbaticals difficult or impossible."[16] The online delivery format seemed ideal as the program was being developed. However, a program offered entirely online did not, in the program developers' estimation, fully meet the needs of their likely audience. Thus, they added the cohort model, focused on residency teams, which are groups of 10 or so students from within the larger cohort. Larson writes that emphasis on the residency teams within the cohort group helps to foster the sense of community "that is so important in adult learners for knowledge creation and satisfaction." And, indeed, program graduates indicate that "the support they derive from each other is huge in their success and satisfaction with the program." Students regularly cite "the connection and community they make with each other when they meet face-to-face" as key to their success.[17]

The blended model proved ideal when the program was initially being considered. Through online course delivery, the Masters in Education Studies program could be offered to a broad and, in many cases, underserved population of working K-12 educators. Yet, the face-to-face connection and sense of community that is clearly a part of student success, particularly for adult learners, was not entirely sacrificed. Instead, community-building opportunities could be built into the larger program with the likely student population's teaching schedules in mind.

Interestingly, though, the M.E.S. program reveals a persistent problem in entirely online delivery. The introduction of synchronous and extensive collaborative online work into an otherwise asynchronous and individual curriculum can present difficulties. Larson notes that "at one point we tried to introduce two separate places for the students to go online.... We wanted them to use a wiki as well as a social networking...system." The additional online activities, which operated outside the standard program course management system, WebCT Vista, and which required some synchronous communication, did not work as well as having learning applications contained entirely within the course management system. Larson does report successful synchronous work with Elluminate, though other synchronous applications tended to be, in Larson's words, "a flop."[18] Elluminate has apparently been particularly useful for course elements that work best synchronously but that do not necessarily require participation by an entire class or that are not a mandatory part of a course, like virtual office hours, small group conversation, and informal student meetings.[19]

In fact, the program does not ask for much collaborative work during the online portions of the curriculum, since the hybrid model provides the opportunity for considerable community building and collaborative work in the face-to-face environment. As Larson maintains, the supportive community that develops in the face-to-face environment carries over into online courses, making mandatory synchronous work online less necessary than might otherwise have been the case.

In addition to the particulars of student success, though, online and hybrid models introduce some interesting broad economic considerations into the picture, and the M.E.S. program is no exception. The cost of the program is listed as $10,400 (all dollar amounts are in Canadian currency). This covers the eight core courses required in the program. Each student is responsible for completing another two courses, the tuition for which varies depending on where and how the courses are taken. The total credit requirement is 30.

Tuition and fees for standard graduate programs is estimated at about $4,500 for full-time fall and winter terms.[20] This estimate includes noninstructional fees such as athletics and recreation and Graduate Student Association health plan dues. Instructional fees alone are closer to $3,500 for fall and winter. Notably, the cost for international students includes a considerable "international student differential fee," which brings full-time tuition for a fall and winter year up to about $8,000 (including instructional and noninstructional fees).

The M.E.S. program cost of \$10,400 is high relative to standard tuition for Canadian students, though it is a bargain relative to international student tuition. And, while the program was designed to serve primarily Alberta educators who, it seemed, were already seeking continuing formal education online from U.S. institutions, the M.E.S. degree has also attracted its share of international students, including those from Africa, the Middle East, and South America. Ultimately, as one University of Alberta administrator notes, evidence indicates that "these students are extremely successful."[21] The program has high retention and completion rates, and students are going back to leadership positions at their own schools.

A STUDENT PERSPECTIVE

Emily Conradt, Graduate Student, Library and Information Science, University of Illinois at Urbana-Champaign

The examples already presented have provided some indication of how individual hybrid classes might look, as well as how an entire degree program might look when premised on the hybrid model. However, we have not yet investigated in depth the student side of the equation. As we have seen, primary motivations for hybridizing courses often include perceived student demand, in addition to administrative or institutional pressure to expand course offerings and faculty desire to offer a more dynamic curriculum that appeals to a variety of learning styles. The success of even the most earnest faculty efforts to innovate, however, inevitably hinges on students' ability to understand and use the technology components of a hybrid course. So let us turn to the student side of the equation.

Emily Conradt was a student in the Masters in Library and Information Science program offered by the University of Illinois at Urbana-Champaign. She graduated in December 2008. The program is built on the hybrid, or blended, model and is composed of fully online courses along with intensive face-to-face class meetings. The online component of the program is highly dynamic, including opportunities for collaborative work and real-time discussion. Classes are required to meet face-to-face only once each semester, though for an entire day, 9 A.M. to 5 P.M. These face-to-face days generally occur midsemester and are coordinated so that students are able to make a single trip to the Urbana-Champaign campus to attend multiple face-to-face meeting days more or less consecutively.

This kind of scheduling clearly reflects the program's stated aim to reach those who are not otherwise able to be on campus regularly. The online education option, or LEEP[22] scheduling option, as it is referred to, is designed expressly for "students who want to attend our well-regarded school [but who] are not always able to relocate to campus. We extend our program to them, and widen our sense of community."[23] Once again we find perceived student demand to be a driving force behind these hybrid programs, with a concurrent sense of broadened institutional community. The impetus to reach an audience that may be geographically diverse—and apparently UIUC online learning programs include students from "Japan, Argentina, Mexico, France, Alaska, and Hawaii"—is similar to what we have seen in the case of the Masters in Education Studies program offered by the University of Alberta. The M.E.S. program, we recall, was developed specifically to attract students who could not attend f2f classes regularly. Neither the UIUC LEEP learning option nor the M.E.S. program, however, chose to go strictly online. Each retains a face-to-face component, opting for infrequent though intensive meeting times in order to preserve the sense of community that comes from f2f interaction.[24]

The LEEP programs offered through UIUC are noteworthy for the varied technologies they include and for the diverse online experiences they offer. In fact, the UIUC online education Web site advertises, "We use advanced technologies that provide live, Web-based instruction: students hear faculty as they speak; they see slides and other graphics, and hear music and audio clips, as the professor discusses them; they 'chat' with the professor and each other." Further, "staff continues to test and refine new technology, ensuring that we remain at the forefront of this exciting educational experience."[25] Part of the intended appeal is clearly an online experience that is dynamic, even cutting edge. Surprisingly though, while the "Technology Requirements" Web page stresses that students should have basic computer competencies (including facility with e-mail, discussion boards, and document preparation), the required hardware is unlikely to ensure student success: "students must have access to the necessary technology at work or at home, including hardware…software, and network connectivity." And, while students are (of course) required to have an Internet connection, the requirements imply that any connection at all will suffice: students must be able to "connect…to a network (via dial-up, broadband, or wireless connection)."[26]

UIUC online education programs operate through Moodle, an open source course management system, and they take advantage of multiple synchronous learning applications, including virtual chat rooms and conferencing. Professors often present visual material in real time, as well. A dial-up connection simply does not allow for this in any reasonable way. Further, one wonders just how feasible working on a computer from a place of employment is likely to be, especially where these kinds of multimedia, synchronous interactions are taking place. Do we presume that a workplace computer will be an adult student's personal computer, a machine that only he or she uses, at a place of business? There is no indication that this is necessarily the case. Common sense—from the faculty and instructional design perspectives, of course—suggests that somebody with a dial-up connection or somebody who must rely on a public computer at a retail job will not choose to enroll for online classes or programs. But such common-sense assumptions need not hold true all of the time. Even when such enrollment is unlikely, unreasonably low-end or unrealistic technology requirements can easily play a factor in poor student engagement, success, and persistence.

So what was the particular experience of Emily Conradt as a student in a LEEP program?

Emily indicates that she enjoyed the hybrid LIS program.[27] The primarily online format, with a few concentrated face-to-face meeting days, worked well for her. She notes further that her fellow students were engaged and supportive. One primary skill she needed to develop early was the ability to manage multiple forms of input at one time. As she describes it, a typical class lecture might be occurring via audio, and the professor might be supplying additional visual material (slides and/or links to related web material), all while students communicate via the Moodle chat feature. In order to participate effectively, Emily had to learn to manage the various input streams. This marks, perhaps, an important part of the profile for a student who is likely to be successful in the online/hybrid format, especially where faculty have designed classes to include considerable synchronous activities that may involve visual, audio, and text-based communication.

Emily is quick to point out that she and her fellow program graduates may represent an ideal set of students. Many are working professionals already, for example, and are focused and conscientious about using time efficiently and productively. Also, the program itself takes care to orient students prior to program coursework beginning. For example, students must attend a 10-day orientation—face-to-face, on campus—before beginning coursework. This 10-day session actually constitutes a for-credit course that is part of the program. Students are required to cover assigned readings beforehand and then to complete a number of activities and written assignments as part of the 10-day course.

Emily describes the 10 days as an "intense experience" that is designed to help students with the technical end of their online work, though it also serves to help students bond early (and in person) so that a real sense of community develops among them. Notably, the initial sense of community that developed from the orientation experience carried through the program for Emily. She notes the "strong sense of community cohesiveness" that she felt with fellow Library and Information Science LEEP students.

In addition to the intensive orientation, the LEEP programs bring students together for face-to-face days during the semester; and, while these days include time for working on class assignments, students are also invited to attend a dinner on campus, organized by the online education program. In other words, the university takes great care in preparing students for success in the program and in fostering a strong sense of community throughout the program. A sense of community, as fundamental to student success in a program of this kind, is also a feature of the M.E.S. program at the University of Alberta.

A strong sense of community among program participants is certainly enhanced by the vigorous efforts on the part of the institution to provide effective support for students, not only in terms of basic technical help and education but also in terms of consistent advising. Technology and library introduction and orientation sessions are offered face-to-face during on-campus meetings days, but continuing technology support and advising sessions are also offered online, which makes perfect sense for a program that occurs almost entirely online. This kind of accessible technology support is especially crucial for the LEEP programs because, to their credit, they involve a number of online applications that allow for extensive student interaction, synchronous and otherwise.

Students might be tasked with presenting information (in real time but online) to the class in the form of a Web site or a wiki, for example. These applications are relatively straightforward, but it is important to provide support for students so that technical barriers do not inhibit learning or class engagement. Emily notes that "the classes are very interactive," which means that the technology involved is generally more complicated than basic online test taking.

The LEEP Web site also makes clear that "Courses may have up to two hours per week of 'live' Internet interaction at a regularly scheduled time."[28] Many institutions that are turning to online and blended learning as a means of growing enrollment may be reluctant to make such declarations, especially when most students indicate that the draw of e-learning is flexibility; however, honest advertising of this sort will better prepare students for success. Retention numbers will surely benefit, too, since students who are more aware of what they are actually signing up for are clearly more likely to have a better learning experience.

It is worth pausing over the student learning experience in this regard because it does have implications for enrollment. When students enjoy a class and feel they have engaged with a community of peers and learned something valuable, they are very likely to communicate this positive experience to friends. Many will publicize such experiences via the Web, as well. Thus, perhaps counterintuitively, while up-front and forthright language about what an online/hybrid course (or program) will entail may discourage a few students from signing up initially, the word-of-mouth advertising of positive student experiences could easily make up the difference.

In fact, positive word-of-mouth advertising is likely to become more and more important as institutions look to attract students by distinguishing themselves from the myriad e-learning offerings now available. To paraphrase Marc Bousquet, writing on the informationalization of higher education in *How the University Works,* big profits from technology were available only to early entrants into the e-learning field. As more schools offer online content, individual schools are less able to extract profit from what might once have been a unique product: computer-based distance education. According to Bousquet, "First adopters of a technology purporting to provide education as information download rake in large profits, because they appear to provide the 'same' service for less." However, this soon becomes "a game that nearly any modest capitalist can join.... As education is stripped down to the provision of information in a larger market share, price competition in that sector intensifies and the rate of profit plummets."[29]

For the thoughtful and ethical institution, this means that flexible learning of all kinds will attract students by virtue of quality instruction, not because a particular delivery mode is unique in the marketplace. It is precisely the positive—or negative—learning experiences that students communicate to one another that will become the distinguishing feature of one e-learning option over another.

No less important for positive student experiences, like Emily's, is the necessity for institutional provisions for those working almost entirely online. Emily cites the library as just one example of a brick-and-mortar resource that must be able to extend its services to online students. The UIUC library catalogue is, of course, online; however, items can also be checked out online and mailed to students. In fact, a University of Illinois campus unit dedicated to distance learning support, called Academic Outreach (part of the Office of Continuing Education), provides, among many other services, document delivery for off-campus and distance ed students.

Institutions must also be prepared to network their library resources with other, sometimes geographically diverse, library systems, so that university library cardholders have borrowing privileges (and are made aware that they have borrowing privileges) at other institutions, including public libraries and other research collections. Emily, for example, made frequent use of "I-Share," a network of 76 Illinois academic and research libraries, which is available to users with a valid ID from any of the participating institutions. Items can be requested via the I-Share catalogue and picked up at the participating institution nearest the patron.

Other kinds of multilibrary networks may operate more locally and include public community libraries. The LINKin network, for example, includes five academic institutions and three large public collections. Library staff who are knowledgeable about these kinds of networked collections and about interlibrary loan programs are an invaluable resource for students and faculty alike. In fact, the growing possibility for ordering research material online and having it delivered via email, in PDF form as opposed to hardcopy, has dramatically altered how students and faculty can undertake scholarly work. Access to multiple collections and delivery modes is particularly meaningful for faculty who do not have direct access to major academic collections but who are nonetheless interested in maintaining active research agendas and staying current in their respective fields. The crucial point is not just that these kinds of services exist but that they are afforded high visibility as institutional resources.

Certain distance learning resources may seem more crucial for entirely online programs as opposed to hybrid programs. Since a blended course will involve some face-to-face time, for example, concerns about library or advising services that reach a geographically dispersed set of students might seem less acute. But notice how this vision is premised on the assumption that a hybrid class will divide its online and face-to-face time in a conventional one-day-on, one-day-off arrangement. Students in a blended class that meets face-to-face every Tuesday but trades its Thursday class time for online work is not likely to require that institutional resources be extended beyond the physical campus.

But what about a hybrid class that splits its time in a different way? What about a class that meets face-to-face, as a traditional class would, for a period of weeks but then transitions to an extended period of online work? Suddenly, the student in the hybrid course comes to resemble much more closely the student in an online course in terms of what resources might need to be in place to enable success. A hybrid course that divides a 16-week semester into 8 f2f weeks and 8 virtual weeks can allow students to leave the physical campus area entirely for an extended period.

Emily sums up her experience in the hybrid LIS program in positive terms: "I have a strong affection for my program and the people in it." She notes, "This is common among the students." Even though the student group that Emily was a part of represents an ideal few relative to the vast numbers of students taking individual online or hybrid classes, clearly something internal to the program itself is working to produce positive learning results. One might even suggest that Emily found herself among motivated and conscientious peers because the LEEP programs have been forthright about the requirements that students will face as mixed-mode learners. Also, part of what we learn from Emily's experience is that technology-rich courses—ones that include regular synchronous meetings; audio, video and text-chat applications; and the use of Web building and wikis—need not present impassable technical barriers for students or for faculty.

Knowledgeable and technically proficient faculty, which ultimately requires a real investment in professional development on the part of the institution, are of course crucial. Of equal value is the focused orientation—face-to-face—that students receive as part of the program, introducing them to the technology that will enable their learning and to the institutional resources (like the library) available even for students who are not physically present on campus for the majority of their degree studies. The key component worth highlighting, and one that is shared by both the LIS program that Emily was a part of and the M.E.S. program at the University of Alberta, is the degree to which a strong sense of community among program participants is actively fostered and enabled.

It is finally worth noting that the cost structure of the hybrid LIS program at the University of Illinois is different from the cost structure of the University of Alberta's M.E.S. program. Whereas the M.E.S. program charges a flat tuition, regardless of whether a student happens to be a Canadian student or is an international student, the UIUC online programs differentiate between in-state and out-of-state student residency. The M.E.S. cost structure thus resembles pricing for entirely online courses, which in most cases charge an in-district rate regardless of the student's geographical location.

The LIS program follows something similar to a traditional-classroom tuition structure. In this case, the total tuition is substantially different for in-state and for out-of-state students. The LEEP Web page estimates total tuition costs for an entire program at $16,280 for an in-state student and $32,120—nearly double—for an out-of-state student.[30] Financial aid opportunities of course affect the number of in-state and out-of-state students, though one wonders how this cost structure aligns with the online education program's stated aims to "widen our sense of community" by providing opportunities to students who cannot regularly attend campus classes.

Ultimately, Emily Conradt reports that she enjoyed the blended learning option, and she clearly benefited from the various opportunities for engagement with faculty and with her peers that it allowed.

VARIATIONS ON A THEME

To conclude this look at a collection of hybrid course and program snapshots, it is useful to stress the great variety one can find in hybrid course design and delivery. In my correspondence with a wide range of college and university educators, what became clear is that variety is the rule. There is no usual hybrid design or standard hybrid delivery strategy. Hybrids take many, many forms and work in many different ways in different disciplines. They arise for different reasons and at different times within the long history of institutions. And they continue to grow beyond their initial beginnings in sometimes surprising ways and for various reasons.

The useful lesson—especially for institutions as a whole—to consider is that hybrids can develop and unfold in diverse ways and yet remain pedagogically sound. They can provide faculty and students with a positive teaching and learning experience and can address institutional needs without becoming mere faddish, stop-gap measures. In other words, what successful variety indicates is that strict, top-down institutional control of hybrid design and development is not a precondition for successful blended learning. Such control may work to create uniformity across a breadth of courses that are developed at a specific time in an institution's history; however, managerial constraints of this kind are useful only for surface matters like course appearance and may be extremely difficult to maintain over the years once a particular learning model gains proponents. Imposing uniformity—or denying variation—is not a necessary condition for the successful development and deployment of hybrid courses.

Remarkable, too, is the number of ways in which hybrids can be different, from the arrangement and division of online and face-to-face activities, to the software and hardware involved, to the complexity of the technology. As we have seen, no consensus exists about what even constitutes a hybrid course. Is a hybrid any class that splits instructional time into 50 percent online and 50 percent face-to-face instruction? Can the percentages differ? Does the non-face-to-face time necessarily have to become online time?

Even in cases where terminology and a hybrid course definition are institutionally negotiated, even contractual, two hybrid courses developed at the same institution by two separate faculty may look very different: one may regularly trade 50 percent face-to-face for online time, while another may retain nearly all the face-to-face seat time and trade f2f days for online work only occasionally.

Some hybrids divide course time fairly evenly between online and f2f activities, though not along a weekly schedule. For example, a graduate course offered at Old Dominion University (ODU) meets for two weeks online (using Blackboard), then meets in person for two weeks, and then goes back to fully online for the final two weeks. This arrangement satisfies residency requirements for the ODU Ph.D. program. Such an arrangement of online and f2f time may in fact show up more often in graduate programs where residency requirements are stricter than for undergraduate degrees. Note again how this arrangement creates the situation in which the traditional student begins to look more like an online student at certain points during the semester in terms of potential need for access to educational resources.

The more common arrangement for hybrids at ODU, however, involves an interesting combination of distance education—conducted via two-way video—and traditional classroom delivery. Distance students meet in a classroom together, though the classroom happens to be at a university satellite campus equipped with video and audio equipment. Students who are not close to a satellite campus can still register for a hybrid class, though they must have a webcam and microphone. The satellite class and the individual students with webcams and microphones are streamed in to an on-campus classroom location, where on-campus students and the professor are physically present. The main campus classroom is equipped with large video screens on which are displayed course content along with images of each of the distance students—the *Hollywood Squares* arrangement, as it has been described. So one class may include students who are physically present together in an on-campus classroom, students who are physically present together but at an off-campus location, and students who are working from a remote personal computer, all interacting in real time.

Though hybrid in the sense that they combine distance education with traditional face-to-face education, and Web-enhanced in that each features full Blackboard support, these hybrids do not trade any seat time for online work. Professor Kathie Gossett, of the Old Dominion English department, indicates that the arrangement works well for the most part, though the school is looking into software that allows the professor to see and control remote computers (i.e., those of the individual distance-learning students) in order to better troubleshoot problems in real time.[31]

ODU hybrid courses are highly structured inasmuch as they are meeting (either in person or via an audio/video bridge) on a regular basis, just as a traditional class would. We may as often find hybrid courses that are scheduled to meet in the traditional, fully face-to-face mode but into which individual faculty have built considerable flexibility. One professor describes his classes as composed of "learning time" as opposed to strictly clock-hour or classroom seat time. Some weeks the class might meet face-to-face as a whole for each of its scheduled meeting times. Other weeks, students may meet in groups, work online, or work in a computer lab or in the library.

The professor schedules "eight hours a week of learning time for a 3 credit course and [we] use the time for what's most effective: if we should meet for the usual scheduled class time because that's what's most useful, we do."[32] The merits of the diverse learning opportunities for students are clear. However, these kinds of classes are not necessarily coded in each term's course schedule as hybrid. The downside is that, going into the class, students are not aware that they will not always meet in the traditional format. With thoughtful course design and with easily accessible support for students who are either intimidated by or unfamiliar with technology, though, the potential is considerable for a class to be successful and highly learner centered and to develop in ways that make sense for that individual class, rather than to unfold in a highly prescriptive manner.

Comments that show up in the learning journals that students keep for each of these classes often indicate a mixture of surprise (usually pleasant) that a class is not what they expected and recognition that learning time can happen outside the classroom. For example, one student writes:

The first few weeks of this class have been very interesting. It's not what I expected it to be, but that's definitely not a bad thing. So far, what I've enjoyed and learned from the most would be the online discussion forums we've set up for each play. This method for discussing the plays seems to encourage more honest, more thought out responses than might arise in class if we were to just break into groups and discuss what we felt about the readings. Online discussion also ensures that no one voice dominates the discussion and everyone can have their say.[33]

Here is another indicative comment: "So far I have really enjoyed the class and my readings. It is [definitely an] unusual approach to learning but sometimes change is good, this is one of those times." And

another: "My expectations were different at the beginning of September [but] any confusion and uncertainty I had felt is no longer at
hand." Clearly, the flexible planning that is fundamental to this kind
of hybrid takes some students initially by surprise. If the student comments are anything to go by though, early feelings of apprehension
soon disappear.

Another interesting variable that shows up among hybrid courses
is exactly how, or whether, they use an official course management
system like Moodle, Blackboard, or Web CT Vista. Where an institution makes it possible, many faculty prefer to provide access to the
online components of a course on an open institutional server—what
amounts to an extensive faculty Web site—rather than through an official course management system. The benefit of this situation is that
faculty enjoy much greater flexibility to personalize the presentation
of material in a way that better reflects their own teaching styles and
approaches than does the more standardized look and feel of a CMS.
A further important consideration here is that in cases where faculty
members are able to use open server space for their online course materials, when students post course work—be it weekly learning journal
entries or major capstone projects—that work is effectively public.

It is unlikely that a random Web surfer would stumble on such work
without seeking it out, but it remains openly accessible nonetheless. I
can, for example, read through the student journals for courses taught
by my colleagues across the country when those journals are hosted
on an open institution server. As long as students are made aware of
the implications, this kind of publication is generally exciting. Often,
students rise to the occasion of having their work made widely accessible to a real audience.

In fact, as is reported in the 2007 Community College Survey of
Student Engagement (CCSSE), LaGuardia Community College saw
an increase between 2005 and 2007 in the percentage of students reporting that their friends and family were supportive of their college
work. During this time, the college made a targeted effort to encourage students to share their e-portfolios with family and friends.[34] The
opportunity for a public audience was certainly not the only factor
that contributed to changing student attitudes beginning in 2005, but it
undoubtedly played a role. And, while growth in the support that students perceived they were getting from friends and family was not, in
the case of LaGuardia Community College, specific to delivery mode,
we can see how opportunities to share work beyond a specific class
could differ significantly for students working entirely in a password-
protected and secure course management system and for those
with access to a more open distribution/publication platform. When

institutions require that online or hybrid content be delivered via an institutionally mandated course management system, the opportunities for wide publication of this kind are limited. Also diminished are opportunities for collaborative efforts across classes at otherwise unrelated institutions.

Of course, CMSs do provide a standardized look, which can certainly help otherwise intimidated students feel more comfortable more quickly as they take classes that feature online components. Many institutions, in fact, cite standardization as a primary benefit—along with security and integration with existing registration and records systems—that can be derived from using a course management system. IT support may also be considerably easier when all faculty members who are teaching online or in the hybrid mode are using, at least as the basis for the online component of a class, the same delivery system.

Those who argue for the need to standardize courses, particularly those delivered entirely online, may not fully apprehend, however, the frequency with which many students take classes from a variety of institutions in order to complete a degree. This is particularly the case for many community college students, who take classes part time and complete a two-year degree in three, four, or five years, some of those years being nonconsecutive. We recall, too, that tuition for online classes is often unaffected by residency, so taking a class from the local college is no more or less expensive, necessarily, than taking a class from a college four states away. Students are facing variation in the courses they take, regardless of whether one institution has mandated a standard e-learning look.

Often, what is gained pedagogically when faculty are able to customize the look and feel of a course and when they are able to include applications beyond institutional course management systems far outweighs the benefits of the standardized look that those course management systems can provide. And, as one educator who prefers to operate outside the official CMS put it: "The main thing we've got that CMSs don't give us is the possibility of a system where the instructor isn't at the center of all the discourse."[35] It is often beneficial, for example, for students to be able to create their own online discussion groups and topics, rather than having to wait for these to be created by the professor.

LESSONS TO LEARN?

Even if variation is the rule, are there any general lessons to learn about effective hybrid course design and delivery? A couple of trends do emerge from the examples we have discussed: hybrid and blended learning situations need to become as transparent as possible, whether high- or low-tech, for student learners, and building a sense of community, online and face-to-face, increases student engagement and thus the potential for meaningful learning to happen in hybrid and blended environments.

We have seen that hybrid courses can involve basic technology like online quizzes, or they can involve more dynamic applications that allow for virtual presentations and real-time collaboration. It is crucial to student success at both ends of this technology continuum that, whatever digital application is in place, it must ultimately be serving a clearly defined—a transparent—pedagogical purpose. An online quiz may be low-tech, but it can play a crucial role in overall course design, providing students and the professor with a regularly recurring assessment tool. Such quizzes can even improve student attendance (both in the physical classroom and virtually) and can thus have a significant impact on engagement and student success. Understanding that these kinds of assignments are not busywork and that they are no less important than other kinds of online work just because they are less technically complicated is crucial if students are to get the most out of them.

In other blended situations we see considerable efforts to encourage a sense of community among learners. This can develop from face-to-face interaction specifically designed to promote a sense of shared learning experiences, or it can unfold virtually when collaborative opportunities are made available to students as part of their online work and when opportunities for the creation of a virtual presence are available for students. We notice, too, that community building in one medium, either face-to-face or online, invariably carries over into the other.

Perhaps what we finally see is that blended learning is a particularly promising horizon on the higher education landscape precisely because it can be so variable in its particulars and yet remain pedagogically sound and produce meaningful, successful learning experiences for all involved.

CHAPTER 6

Technology: Trending to Community and Collaboration

As we have seen, technology encompasses a wide variety of applications, some dynamic, rich, and complex, others straightforward and simple. And, again, while terms like "dynamic" and "rich" may carry greater positive connotations than terms like "straightforward" and "simple," which are negatively charged in some contexts, no such value judgment is implied here. Terms like "high" and "low" are merely descriptive, useful in noting the range of technologies that show up, or that might show up, in hybrid and blended classes. What ultimately matters is not what online applications are being used but how they are being used.

The discussion in this chapter does tend to focus on those technologies that are less likely to figure as part of blended learning classes already, including applications outside of standard course management system and tools beyond basic assessment. As we have seen in the various examples of hybrids discussed earlier, many faculty who start by using relatively straightforward course management tools will find themselves at some point interested in expanding the scope of the online work that their students are doing. And addressing more abstract pedagogical aims—like improved critical thinking, digital literacy, and effective collaboration—often requires more complex approaches. Though we noted earlier that going hybrid need not, by necessity, become a technology-intensive endeavor, curricular redesign that includes the development of hybrid courses does present the opportunity for truly re-imagined teaching.

The blended model may provide faculty with the ideal platform to include more ambitious technologies in their classes and to direct those technologies to the increasingly visible educational goals of collaboration and communal content creation. Because the hybrid model preserves face-to-face interaction—a much better medium for introducing and troubleshooting dynamic online learning tools—many faculty may discover the opportunity that they have been waiting for to use interesting technology in their classes without having to present and troubleshoot that technology in an entirely virtual setting.

One of the most widely visible learning objectives—and one that employers are more and more identifying as crucial for newly degreed hires—is collaboration. This term has been the buzzword of 21st-century education. The 2008 *National Survey of Student Engagement* (NSSE),[1] for example, uses as one of its primary student engagement benchmarks "active and collaborative learning." According to NSSE, "Collaborating with others in solving problems prepares students to deal with the messy, unscripted problems they will encounter daily, both during and after college." The survey also suggests that "the online setting may offer more opportunities for collaboration and faculty who teach online courses may be more intentional about fostering active learning experiences."[2]

The implication in the NSSE report—and this appears regularly in such studies—is that the online environment, despite usually being stereotyped as dehumanized and isolating, may actually be the ideal setting for bringing students together as collaborative learners. "Integrating technology-enhanced courses into the curriculum for all students might have some salutary effects" when it comes to addressing problems of student engagement and thus success.[3]

No less, we are seeing that collaboration and social knowledge construction are becoming valuable workplace assets. In their book *Wikinomics*, Don Tapscott and Anthony D. Williams describe "profound changes" in the new global economy. They note that "powerful new models of production based on community, collaboration, and self-organization, rather than hierarchy and control" are emerging as the dominant trend in business.[4] Where once corporations were careful to protect their intellectual property and to rely solely on in-house talent for value creation, we now see examples of mass collaboration and open intellectual property as the cornerstones for successful business development.

In higher education, too, we are seeing the ideals of openness prevail. The Massachusetts Institute of Technology (MIT), for example, provides open access to a large portion of its course content and materials through the OpenCourseWare initiative (OCW): "OCW is a web-based publication of virtually all MIT course content. OCW is open and available to the world and is a permanent MIT activity."[5] MIT is part of the Open Courseware Consortium, an international group of colleges and universities that has made course materials freely available on the Web. The consortium's stated mission is to "advance education and empower people worldwide through opencourseware."[6] Member Web sites are clear to point out, though, that what they offer is simply course material, not an actual college course that a student can take to earn credit.

Having students work in collaborative, knowledge-sharing modes is crucial to their future success in careers that are more and more likely to demand of them the skill to work effectively in collaborative settings and to understand that even a simple document can emerge from a multistage process of editing and sharing. We do not need to abandon the traditional essay or the process of its creation as crucial components of assessing student achievement in higher education; rather, we need to expose students to a diversity of ways in which an essay or other written work might come into being. More than just the product of an individual student typing away in a word processing program, an essay can as easily unfold through a process of sharing, revising, and basic editing through Google Docs or a wiki. In fact, when the essay for English class of today becomes the professional text of tomorrow, it is more and more likely to have emerged from a process of collaborative document sharing and creation than from the keyboard of a single individual.

Eileen Connell, an e-media development editor with the publisher W. W. Norton, describes the typical process for document collaboration in her workplace. Employees work with Google Sites, a free Web and wiki application that allows for document sharing:

We use google sites to create "profiles" (basically, plans) for our e-media products. They are shared with everyone on the team: book editor, emedia editor, emedia editor colleagues, web designers, marketing associate, director of emedia, etc. Some people have only "viewing" privileges and others are permitted to edit and add to the document. We also use google sites to post ideas for future emedia, notes from our meetings, charts of what comparable products our competitors offer, etc.[7]

The Google Sites Web site includes positive commentary from other users, indicative of how important document collaboration has become for many businesses. For example: "Google Sites has revolutionized the way we communicate with our clients and with our team members."[8] Clearly, the student who comes into a professional landscape like this having had some exposure to shared document circulation and creation will be much more comfortable and effective.

Successful collaboration, in the classroom and in the workplace, is often a difficult goal to achieve, however. This is probably why it does not show up as often as we might hope in college curricula, especially within the online environment. Even NSSE results indicate that, while collaborative learning remains a prized ideal, only 16 percent of student survey respondents who were in their first year of college reported that they "Discussed or completed an assignment using a 'synchronous' tool like instant messenger, online chat, video conference, etc."[9]

Collaborative learning may certainly still unfold through asynchronous means, like e-mail, but it seems reasonable to assume that increased real-time communication by collaborative learners could only deepen the experience. So if we embrace this early period in hybrid learning as a time to truly re-see how the practical activities of teaching can align with broad, 21st-century pedagogic goals, what might some of the digital applications we could use actually look like in action?

COURSE MANAGEMENT SYSTEMS: BUILDING VIRTUAL PRESENCE

Blackboard is now the dominant player in the field of course management systems, though other systems are available (including WebCT Vista and Moodle). Each of these systems offers more or less the same set of features. While it is important to understand local variations, for our purposes here the similarities are more important than the differences. And, while there are many features available in each of these course management systems that educators can readily use to manage a hybrid course (e.g., a grade book or class roster), a couple of features with much more direct implications for fostering student engagement through community building are worth identifying specifically. First, we look at ways to establish a virtual presence.

Of course, it may seem that establishing an online presence as part of a hybrid class might be less crucial than would be the case for a class occurring entirely online. But, even when students have the opportunity to meet regularly face-to-face, as a group, it is still important to provide each student with the opportunity to create a dynamic online self. On a practical level, providing students the opportunity to establish a virtual presence helps them to feel a sense of integration between the f2f and online components of a class. They can feel present in both components.

As we know from many student engagement studies, feeling connected is crucial for student success. And feeling connected means being more than a number. Fortunately, in most course management systems students are not identified purely by number, although educators and students alike will notice how names are often accompanied by a student PIN of some kind. Without a means to build an online identity and to form a substantial connection to the virtual portion of a hybrid class, many students disconnect. One student, whose comment is included in the *2008 NSSE*, notes that one of the most important aspects of his time at college was that "I was a person to so many people, not a number."[10]

Without some form of online identity that they have had a hand in creating, students may easily feel they are, really, just a number, their name operating more as a placeholder than a personal identifier of any meaningful kind. Equally important is that faculty establish an online identity beyond their name as well (which can itself become a placeholder, unfortunately privileged in the CMS naming scheme), even though they embody themselves regularly in the physical classroom. Carrying that physically embodied presence into the online environment is crucial. Experiential and quantitative data both suggest that "developing relationships—with other students, faculty, and staff—is a significant contributor to student success."[11]

A few simple tools can help with this kind of relationship building. We will see, though, that even in situations where the practical technology remains straightforward, the broader implications can be much more complicated. This is one reason that attention across higher education constituencies needs to be paid now to blended learning.

The community-building examples we will look at first are basic enough: each student can be required to build a course management system homepage, and faculty can quite easily add video of themselves throughout a course.

Building an individual homepage, as in Blackboard, for example, is a task that my own students take on in the first week of my online and hybrid courses. I encourage students to be creative, to include a picture (very important for community building), and to think of their Web page as the tool that will make a first impression on the rest of the class. Asking students to respond to specific questions when they build their homepages ("what's your favorite movie?" or "what book did you last read?") sets up the next crucial step, which is to have students look at each others' homepages and, I hope, to find points of connection or shared interests that are not necessarily class related.[12]

We may take time to discuss in class what kinds of things students have written on their homepages and to look at pictures that people have chosen to post. We also explore shared likes or dislikes that students have discovered with their classmates. This rather simple exercise helps to initiate a sense of community that exists both in the class and online. It also helps to reinforce that the online identity is not separate from the classroom identity. Nor is the online self meant to be an experiment or façade, as can often be the case (sometimes usefully) when users create identities in social networking or virtual world applications. It can be interesting to pose virtually as the opposite gender in some cases, for example. But that is not the point in developing an online presence for my blended classes. Especially in the hybrid mode, a sense of community may develop for the group in the face-to-face setting while the online component remains an isolating place to work if we do not take steps to extend the physical classroom self into the virtual arena.

Having thus encouraged students to consider their presence in the face-to-face classroom and also in our online classroom, it makes sense for me as the educator to build my online presence as well, beyond the text-based communication that dominates so much of online teaching. Short video clips are an easy way to embody myself virtually so that the online me does not become a separate entity from the classroom me.

In some cases, institutional production services help faculty to produce high-quality, professional video of themselves. However, the lo-fi approach might actually do a better job of providing the humanizing element we are looking for. In fact, students, in my experience, will understand that you are recording on your own, with a webcam and your office computer. They are not looking for professional video work. They are looking for you, the human you, in the online environment. Again, seeing you click, look at the computer, look at the webcam, look back at the computer, then finally say what you, um, have to, um, say... this all may produce a very real and approachable online identity (if a somewhat comical one), which is ultimately what we are going for. The do-it-yourself, or DIY, approach may be preferable in these cases to more professional efforts, even if it produces less pristine results.[13]

Enabling a sense of community across the various media that make up the blended environment by creating an online presence for students (through building personal homepages) and for faculty (by including video clips in online material) is fairly straightforward. From the faculty and institutional side of things, however, it may create a significant problem, one that goes straight to the heart of how blended course design and delivery are handled at the institutional level.

When it comes to fully online courses, it is often the case that the initial development of a course is undertaken as a paid project or work-for-hire. The work-for-hire project is completed by one faculty member or perhaps by a small group. Because the course is built as a work for hire, the intellectual property of that course rests not with the faculty who designed it and who would presumably teach it but with the institution that paid for it. Faculty may not see the implications of this arrangement at the time of development, especially at an institution that is just beginning to formally grow a set of online offerings. It is vital to consider whether hybrid courses will be similarly developed as works for hire by faculty who are compensated for the task, rather than as part of curricular development of the more traditional sort: faculty undertake the revision and development of courses as part of their normal professional duties. This traditional curricular work is not compensated beyond a faculty member's regular pay, and intellectual property ownership of the curricular material rests with the faculty member, not with the institution.

Recall that the practical matter under discussion here is simply adding faculty video to a course. How did this become an issue of intellectual property rights? If faculty build video of themselves into a course, recalling that this is clearly a beneficial pedagogic strategy, then how does an institution exercise its intellectual property rights over that course and have it taught by a different faculty member? It would be odd, to say the least, to have video of a professor other than the one who is actually teaching the class showing up throughout an online or hybrid course. If major revisions are required, to either remove or replace video throughout a course, is that work compensated? And is it compensated each and every time a different faculty member has to undertake it? Obviously, it would be administratively easier to mandate that video not be included as part of online content at all.

We thus face the possibility that institutional policies about course content could trump pedagogically minded course design decisions. This problem is similar to that which arises when we seek the illusory benefits that some believe to inhere in having online and hybrid offerings follow a standardized look. Basically, we have course content decisions managed outside individual faculty hands.

This tension surrounding course content, control, and management— arising even from the seemingly simplest of practical course design examples—forms the backdrop for discussion of almost all kinds of online applications, whether they appear in strictly online courses or in the blended environment. Ultimately, how will the pedagogical benefits of certain digital applications be weighed against the demands they place on institutional resources and the complications they produce in terms of managing and maintaining curricula? We can hope that institutional thinking will favor pedagogy over managerial convenience.

BLOGS: A PUBLIC SPHERE IN THE CLASSROOM

Blogs—short for weblogs—are old news when it comes to popular use and acceptance. A weblog is simply a Web site that allows its user (generally the creator of the blog) to enter posts, or weblog entries, on whatever subject suits his or her fancy. Posts can be frequent or infrequent. And, while weblogs started as primarily text-based, they now afford bloggers the opportunity to include audio and video. Bloggers can even post from cell phones and other mobile devices.

Perhaps lost in the current focus on content, be it text, audio, or video, is the earliest impetus behind blogs: to share Web links to content other than what the blogger is actually producing. In this sense, blogs were originally, and in some cases still are, designed to create assemblages, or linkages, among many users and content producers. The focus on communal knowledge production has, to some degree, been lost with the contemporary focus on blogs as more akin to newspapers or magazines—content providers, rather than hyperlinking tools.

Ideally, though, as educational tools, blogs enable a kind of public sphere of discussion and debate—though the sphere in each case might be limited to a single class. As Aaron Barlow writes in his *Blogging America*, "no blog exists alone...each is part of a greater conversation that includes comments, links, and other blogs."[14] This is exactly the kind of interconnectedness and multiplicity we might take advantage of by using blogs in the blended learning setting.

Blogs now are fairly ubiquitous. Millions of people have them and blog regularly. Millions more create a blog but then never use it. The word "blog" is both noun and verb. In fact, in 2004, the dictionary publisher Merriam-Webster selected "blog" as its top word of the year, and "blog" has been included in Merriam-Webster's print dictionary since 2005.[15] In 2006, *Time* named "You" as its "Person of the Year," a nod to the power of Web tools like blogs to give the everyday Joe a public voice. As Lev Grossman enthusiastically noted, "for seizing the reins of the global media, for founding and framing the new digital democracy, for working for nothing and beating the pros at their own game, TIME's Person of the Year for 2006 is you."[16]

Blogs have become so much an accepted part of the larger media landscape that we often hear established news outlets make reference to broad blogging communities, like conservative bloggers or liberal bloggers. Neither category is static, of course, but the notion of a like-minded group that voices publicly accessible opinions—through blogs—provides many mainstream media outlets with a reference point for how public events circulate within a certain kind of community.

Most people these days know what a blog is, though they may not actually blog themselves. Indeed, blogs have become so numerous that we now have a related term, the blogosphere. Tapscott and Williams describe the blogosphere as a "vociferous stream of dialogue and debate."[17] This virtual space includes the millions of individual blogs that exist but also connotes their interconnectedness, the sum of the community, or communities, beyond the individual constituent parts.

It is in this latter sense, as a sphere of public commentary, that blogs can be particularly valuable. In its most basic use, a weblog that a student keeps for class is little different from a traditional learning journal of the type that educators have long been requiring of students. An ongoing writing journal is certainly useful in and of itself. It asks the writer to sustain engagement over a long period (a semester, for example) by requiring regular journal entries, even if each individual entry need not be extensive. It can also free the writer from the formal and rhetorical constraints of the extended argumentative essay. A journal entry does not necessarily require a fully worked out thesis, for example, or completely elaborated evidence. A writing journal may, in fact, contain more questions than answers.

Migrating the traditional writing journal to the Web, to a blog, does not change its basic character. It does, however, make the journal public. By thinking in terms of a class blogosphere, a public arena, rather than thinking in terms of individual student journals, we see the potential to build a sense of class community. We can recognize and encourage a sense of connectedness among student bloggers.

Having students set up and use a weblog is relatively easy. Numerous free utilities, from Wordpress (at wordpress.com) to Blogger (at blogger.com) guide users through a basic registration and set-up process, and they end up with a unique weblog address, something like myname.blogspot.com. Having a little bit of virtual territory is often exciting for students (as for users generally), since it provides the space to build a virtual, and public, identity. Certainly this element of identity creation is enticing for many, as is the opportunity to have a public voice.

The important part of blogs as spaces for identity creation is, of course, their public nature. This aspect of being able to write in a public space is ideal for encouraging students to consider issues of voice, tone, and style, inasmuch as anybody might be reading what they write and post to their weblogs. In my experience, students have even received comments on their blogs from complete strangers who have stumbled upon the student's work. It is, in fact, this commenting feature that provides the community-building opportunities presented by weblogs. By having students actively read and comment on one another's blog posts, we can develop that sense of a communal virtual space, a micro-blogosphere, and micro-public sphere.

Blogs may be most promising in the classroom less for their use as purely content production tools than for the way in which they can help students connect to a public sphere, a multivoiced dialogue outside the classroom and for the way in which blog features can be used to create a micro-blogosphere for an individual class. The comment feature becomes extremely important as we encourage continuing dialogues among students in a class.

Barlow has noted that blogs have been part of the "taking back of the public sphere [from] commercial new media."[18] And Tapscott and Williams write that, for too long, prior to Web tools like blogs, "too many people were bypassed in the circulation of knowledge, power, and capital and thus participated at the economy's margins."[19] One hopes that, by encouraging students to work toward a class blogosphere (rather than just a brimming individual blog of their own), we can enable students to co-create an expertise with their peers that might otherwise remain the purview of the professor. As Barlow notes, "the fact of expertise established outside of the blogs...is always trumped by expertise *demonstrated* through the blogs."[20] Students are especially eager for opportunities to demonstrate expertise because—as students—they are rarely accorded any respect for already having it.

WIKIS: THE ART OF MANAGING COLLABORATION

As perhaps the most visible wiki—Wikipedia—tells us, the word "wiki" is Hawaiian for "fast." A wiki is a Web site that can be quickly, or at least easily, accessed, edited, and expanded by a collaborative group of users. Wikis enable quick collaboration. Used effectively, wikis transform passive Web site visitors into active Web site contributors. Wikis thus provide an ideal educational tool, since they depend on collaborative efforts. And, as Web-based applications, wikis can also feature more than just text. They can include audio, still graphics, and motion video, along with links to material inside the wiki and beyond.

Wikipedia provides an ideal example of how wikis are unique in their operation: content is created and edited almost entirely by users. According to Wikipedia itself, "Wikipedia is written collaboratively by volunteers from all around the world; anyone can edit it."[21]

Perhaps the most interesting aspect of a wiki that is as large as Wikipedia is the degree to which content is not just created by the community of users but actually vetted largely by that community, as well. Some might wonder how an open project like Wikipedia, editable by any-body who happens to be online, can be even remotely reliable. As the site admits, many new entries in the wiki encyclopedia are not, in fact, that reliable; "older articles tend to be more comprehensive and bal-anced, while newer articles more frequently contain significant mis-information, unencyclopedic content, or vandalism."[22] Newer entries may show a marked degree of bias or contain incorrect material. Only after enough time has passed for multiple users—perhaps hundreds or thousands—to correct mistakes and even the tone might a Wikipedia entry constitute a reliable source. Also, users can tag any entry they feel contains debatable or inaccurate information. As a fail-safe, a system of prior versions of each entry—a kind of change-tracking method—allows previous versions of a Wikipedia entry to be recalled in case new changes do more harm than good, intentionally or otherwise.[23]

Wikipedia, while open and collaborative, is not a democracy, as the site points out. In other words, it is not a platform for unlimited and unrestricted free speech. Actually, quite the contrary is true. A quick glance through Wikipedia's "About" materials—which include Wiki-pedia's history and its contributor policies—reveals that Wikipedia's mission is fairly narrow in scope: it aims, as does a quality print en-cyclopedia, to reflect and collect existing knowledge. It is not a soap-box. As such, in addition to the thousands and thousands of volunteer users who act as editors to ensure the accuracy of Wikipedia informa-tion, a much smaller number of administrators is able to handle cases of wiki vandalism, blatant advertising, defamation, or other disruptive behavior.

How do other wikis handle the potential problems inherent in an open system of this sort? One good example is provided by WikiTravel, which bills itself as "a free, up-to-date, complete and reliable world-wide travel guide."[24] This wiki is big (though nothing like Wikipedia), but it makes explicit that casual users can add to—and alter—the wiki with ease. WikiTravel stresses that the site is entirely reader-created and that to contribute you do not have to be an expert. WikiTravel is forward with its invitation to edit content: "You have as much right to edit anything on WikiTravel as anyone else does. Don't bother asking whether it's all right to edit something. It is!"[25] So what keeps the wiki from becoming a shambles, a mishmash of bad information, blatant self-promotion, profanity for the sake of profanity, and so on? Aside from a team of administrators (who, according to WikiTravel, will only step in for the most intractable of problems), what polices the wiki is the social body of its contributors. As much as WikiTravel stresses that anybody can add and edit content, it goes to equal lengths to stress that the wiki community can deal with problems much more effectively than an intrusive authority that operates outside of the community.

Even in the case of a user ban, which WikiTravel indicates is an extreme last resort, "someone needs to nominate the user...for banning on the WikiTravel: user ban nominations page." Administrators handle the technical side of the ban, but they do not initiate the procedure. WikiTravel makes clear that such drastic measures as user bans "are *embarrassing*, because they are an admission that our community is not strong, patient, and professional enough to deal with unwanted edits using the simple freedom built into the Wiki way."[26] Trust is placed in the community, the social body, of the wiki.

So, as with weblogs, one of the most interesting educational aspects of wikis is not the technology per se. Nor is it simply students learning the technical skills of producing content with wikis (e.g., how to add new pages, how to add text and image, how to edit). What is particularly worth foregrounding when we include wiki projects in blended learning situations is exactly how communal knowledge is created— the social aspect of it all. How does a collaborative group manage itself, uphold guidelines, craft shared vision and goals, and deal with problem contributions?

In this sense, a classroom wiki project may be much more open and democratic than the wiki most everybody knows about, Wikipedia. Students may have to consider for themselves and put into practice a system of collaboration that allows for multiple voices and perspectives to enter the discussion. Students may also have to experience and deal with a member of the group who contributes inaccurate information, or who makes inappropriate changes to others' content, or— worst-case scenario—who does not take the assignment seriously and ultimately vandalizes the wiki with inappropriate tone or content, off-color or irrelevant material, or overly personal soap box diatribe.[27]

Even working in small groups—say, three, four, or five people collaborating on a wiki—students will have to negotiate what Wikipedia terms "consensus as collective thought." This concept may be a very new experience for many students. Recall, too, that we are talking about students from potentially diverse backgrounds, not just the traditional college-age learner who has come straight out of high school. Students will ideally have to experience the degree to which group work often involves compromise, collaborative goal setting, and the delegation of duties. Students will also see how a social body polices itself, even if the social contract in this case extends to just a handful of students.

The real challenge and the real learning opportunity presented by wikis is not understanding their technical aspects but rather managing diversity. And this is most certainly a 21st-century learning goal that will become more and more important. As James West and Margaret West have written, "Students who engage in online collaboration and wiki work during their education will be well prepared for the challenges of the virtual workplace."[28]

But what is true for wikis is equally true for any other learning tool: as West and West argue, "When framed well, wiki projects can support effective pedagogy and can promote knowledge construction, critical thinking, and real-world application of skills and concepts."[29] The key component here, the one upon which learning outcomes ultimately rest, is, of course, the idea of wiki projects being framed well. In other words, to return to our most basic premise, wikis as a technology need to be transparent; they need to be presented as a classroom tool that overcomes a significant problem or that allows us to do something educationally better than what we had been doing before.

Making transparent for all involved the reason for using wikis in a course will undoubtedly make the effectiveness of the technology that much more substantial, especially as we attempt to direct interest away from technology for its own sake and toward technology as a tool for letting us explore important social or cultural phenomena. Students who are encouraged to think about the social and collaborative dynamics of building a wiki with classmates are much less inclined to understand it as merely a computer assignment.

A further set of digital tools can facilitate collaborative efforts, though with a focus less on content creation and more on content sharing.

SOCIAL BOOKMARKING: SHARING CONTENT AND COMMUNITY

To bookmark a page on the Web has, until recently, been a fairly private and personal activity: you find something on the Web that you might like to refer to later, so you add it to your personal bookmarks. In Mozilla's Firefox browser, there is a Bookmarks tab, and in Microsoft's Internet Explorer browser you will find a Favorites tab. They work pretty much the same way. You can organize and manage your favorites, but they remain personal to you.

Imagine, however, that you could share your bookmarks, your favorites, with a group of friends or colleagues. Anytime you find interesting or useful content on the Web, you update your personal bookmarks, and all of your group members are alerted to the update. When these folks find and bookmark content, you are similarly updated. This turns the once fairly personal and private act of bookmarking from the virtual equivalent of dog-earing pages in your copy of a book to the virtual equivalent of dog-earing pages in everybody's copy of that book. It becomes a social and communal act of knowledge sharing.

Another useful aspect of social bookmarking is that it allows users to tag content using particular keywords. For example, if I am browsing the Web for data on graduation rates and come across some interesting or useful content, I can bookmark it and also add keywords to what I have found (maybe "education," "graduation," and "two-year schools"). These tags help to form interconnections among my various bookmarks, ones that I have tagged with a similar keyword. So all of my bookmarks tagged with "education" can be grouped together, for example. Applying multiple tags to bookmarked content that I find multiplies the potential interconnections among my bookmarks. Perhaps more pointedly, from the social perspective of social bookmarking, tagging bookmarks with keywords allows me to find what other users have similarly tagged, and I can share, within a group of users that can be large or small, bookmarks to content that is likely to be of interest because it shares the same keyword tag. Some have described this as "public annotation."[30]

The system of social or collaborative tagging also sets up an interesting kind of vocabulary for the participant group: a folksonomy. This is a language set that is produced and developed by users. A folksonomy is bottom-up and changes fluidly with user activity. When we imagine social bookmarking as a potential feature of blended or hybrid learning we begin to see the valuable context it sets up for investigating how language itself operates, circulating among a group of users and changing according to their activities.

The innumerable social bookmarking sites available to users operate much like other kinds of social software: you sign up and receive a personal webspace that is provided through the application, and others can follow your bookmarks by either visiting your site or by subscribing and receiving updates automatically every time you bookmark, or tag, something interesting. Many utilities allow you to add a button to your favorite Web browser so that you can bookmark on the fly. The point is less about a group following one individual's bookmarking, though, and more about that entire group generating and sharing a set of related bookmarks. As one social bookmarking application—called Delicious—highlights, "With emphasis on the power of the community, [social bookmarking] greatly improves how people discover, remember and share on the Internet."[31]

Delicious is actually one of the most visible social bookmarking applications. It describes itself as "The tastiest bookmarks on the web."

Here are a few other social bookmarking applications, along with a sampling of the advertising rhetoric associated with each:

- Digg (http://digg.com/): "Digg is a place for people to discover and share content from anywhere on the web...we're here to provide a place where people can collectively determine the value of content and we're changing the way people consume information online."
- Reddit (http://www.reddit.com/): "Reddit is a source for what's new and popular online. Vote on links that you like or dislike and help decide what's popular, or submit your own!"
- Newsvine (http://www.newsvine.com/): "Updated continuously by citizens like you, Newsvine is an instant reflection of what the world is talking about at any given moment."
- Diigo (http://www.diigo.com/): This used to be Furl. Diigo allows users to highlight pieces of content as they browse the web and attach their own virtual sticky notes to Web pages. These annotations show up for the user every time he or she returns to the page. Diigo is also a social bookmarking and content site: "With every Diigo user tagging and annotating pages online, the Diigo community has collectively created a wonderful repository of quality content, filtered and annotated by the community, on almost any subject you may be interested in."

What is interesting about the kind of language associated with each of these applications as they present themselves on the Web is the degree to which the activity of social bookmarking is figured as citizens creating networks among themselves through a grassroots model of community building. We recall, perhaps, the similar civic rhetoric found in ESPN's SportsNation. This grassroots image does not mean, though, that big business does not have a hand in it all. Delicious, for example, was started in 2003 by Joshua Schachter but acquired by Yahoo! in 2005.

An equally noteworthy activity related to bookmarking and made evident in the rhetoric attached to social bookmarking sites involves voting on or recommending content for other users. As the Digg Web site declares, "people can collectively determine the value of content."[32] Delicious also advertises that it can "show you the most popular bookmarks being saved right now across many areas of interest," and the Delicious homepage "shows you the hottest bookmarks on Delicious right now."[33]

As with blogs and wikis, we find that social bookmarking as a digital activity has interesting applications for a hybrid class or e-learning situation. Individual students could be asked to keep a weblog, create a wiki, or register for a social bookmarking account and begin marking their favorite places and content on the Web. Bookmarking could become even more assignment-specific if students are asked to bookmark with a view to producing a research essay or a presentation, for example. Diigo's highlighting feature could also be useful, at least for each individual student, in this regard.

But, beyond each digital tool and its use by an individual student, we find considerable opportunities for encouraging student collaboration and thus building class community. It would seem useful to have students use applications like Digg or Delicious, not just to reflect their own particular interests or as complements to their individual assignments but rather to actively share their bookmarks, comment on one another's blog posts, and reflect on exactly how their collaborative work on a wiki unfolds. What keeps it all from going off the rails?

The voting aspect of social bookmarking provides a nice, simple strategy for encouraging students to feel that they are making decisions as a group, a small social body. Sites like Digg, for example, allow users to bookmark what they feel is interesting content and then to rate other bookmarks: "participate in the collaborative editorial process by Digging the stuff that you like best."[34] The alternative is (somewhat confusingly) not to Digg but to Bury bookmarked content that is either uninteresting or that is no longer accessible on the Web. As with other social media, the system works best and is most productive when a social body is involved. And, of course, an individual can share his or her bookmarks with others, creating a network of potentially like-minded folks. The group acts as a sort of filtering mechanism. As Meredith Farkas notes, voting and recommendation systems "have an undeniable power to help users make decisions."[35]

The idea of a class-based Delicious account to which students contribute bookmarks, vote on and evaluate bookmarked content, and tag bookmarks to develop interconnections is especially promising for building community and for exposing students to socially produced knowledge. The idea of a folksonomy that students in a given class develop for themselves, for example, seems well suited to a pedagogy that encourages students to take responsibility for their own learning.

SECOND LIFE: REAL LEARNING IN A VIRTUAL WORLD

Second Life is a 3-D immersive world, divided into parcels of virtual land called islands, in which users create for themselves avatars, or digital selves. These can be as flamboyant and fanciful, or as proper and true to life, as one prefers. Users, through their avatars, can interact with the virtual world of Second Life and of course with one another, using a text-based instant messaging tool or by using Second Life's voice-over-Internet-protocol audio function. Second Life bills itself as an "online 3D world imagined and created by its Residents."[36]

A virtual world like Second Life, because it shares a visual dynamic in common with online games, is often identified as a MMORPG: a massively multiplayer online role-playing game. Another form of this acronym is MMOG, massively multiplayer online game. These networked games allow many players, geographically dispersed, to participate in the game at any one time; Disney's *Pirates of the Caribbean*, which we looked at in chapter 3, is a good example of an online multiplayer game, though it is just one among many. The basic similarity these games share, however, is the goal-driven nature of the game itself. Most games are composed of a series of quests or adventures. As such, there will always be an underlying narrative in which gamers are participating, though user participants may, through their playing of the game, shape that narrative to some degree. In fact, many narratives may be unfolding at any given time as each player or group of players pursues individual quest goals within the larger narrative world of the game.

The goal-oriented nature of most MMORPGs is what they tend to share in common. But it is also what makes a virtual world like Second Life substantially different. In the virtual space of Second Life, there is no foundational narrative, no existing content that necessarily motivates or enables action on the part of users. This is, of course, where the educational possibilities of virtual environments are so exciting, but it is also where the broad investment of institutional support is so crucial.

While an application like Second Life bills itself as produced, for the most part, by resident users themselves, the virtual building and scripting required to produce professional looking content are fairly complex. Basic object creation in Second Life is simple enough, but there are only so many virtual cubes and spheres that one avatar needs. More complicated building and texturing requires considerable time, effort, and expertise. Certainly, some faculty will be able and motivated to invest the energy it takes to become proficient in Second Life's building procedures. Alternately, professionally constructed content can be purchased—often built to order—if institutional funding is in place to support such things. Scripting, or programming objects so that they do something, requires knowledge of Second Life's proprietary scripting language, Linden Scripting Language (LSL). As with building, professionals are available for hire to script complicated animations and virtual interactivity, though a few Web-based utilities make basic scripting manageable for the average user.[37] For most teachers, the interactive and social aspects of Second Life are likely to seem most promising, not the opportunity to produce Second Life content. The primary concern is likely to be how an application like Second Life can enable a dynamic and real-time interactivity among students who are not actually face-to-face.

A virtual world like Second Life is, in some ways, just a dynamic and three-dimensional version of the Web. Where we might normally browse a Web page or even build our own Web sites, Second Life virtualizes the user—so you are not browsing the Web; rather, your avatar is literally walking through the built spaces in Second Life. And what fills those spaces includes everything from virtual renditions of physical retail stores to educational spaces complete with virtual copies of physical campuses to virtual meeting places for profit and nonprofit organizations alike.

For example, the shoemaker Reebok enjoyed real success through its virtual store in Second Life. Users could create customized virtual shoes. The virtual Reebok store reportedly distributed some 27,000 pairs of shoes in the first 10 weeks of its Second Life presence.[38] Many companies, like Reebok, are hoping that brand exposure in the virtual world will lead to increased sales in the real world. Despite some individual successes in this regard, however, the jury is still out on whether major investment in a Second Life presence will pay off in real sales. Raz Schionning, who was responsible for American Apparel's 2006 move into Second Life, admits, "I'm not really sold on it yet." Retailers are recognizing that a virtual presence in Second Life, in the form of a billboard or Second Life event sponsorship, is more akin to brand exposure as it happens in the real world than it is to e-commerce. Joseph Laszlo, an analyst with Jupiter Research, notes that when it comes to creating and maintaining a brand presence in Second Life, "You actually have to think more like a bricks-and-mortar retailer than a virtual retailer."[39]

Many colleges and universities have invested in building a Second Life presence for themselves, in some cases creating a virtual duplicate of a physical campus. Widespread buy-in across higher education has not yet happened, though. Tightening budgets and lack of broad awareness are just two reasons, among many, that schools have not staked out some virtual territory. Some kind of Web presence is a given for institutions of higher learning, however, and a similarly widespread virtual presence in Second Life may also emerge in the near future.

The results for institutions that have made a serious commitment to create, develop, and maintain a Second Life presence are quite striking in many cases, however. Bradley University, for example, opened its Second Life space to visitors in March 2008. The list of virtual activities and exhibits that took place as part of the official opening suggests just how closely the virtual Bradley is meant to mirror the actual Bradley. Visitors to the virtual space could check out the campus grounds, the Student Center (first and second floors), Cullom-Davis Library, the multistory Education and Health Sciences building, the Slane Communication and Fine Arts building, and the Robertson Memorial Fieldhouse.[40] Visit Bradley in Second Life and you do feel as though you are visiting an actual university campus. In fact, it is this immersive element that makes Second Life such a promising tool for teaching in disciplines that involve spatial relations, including obvious examples like architecture but also fields as diverse as fashion design (you can stage and choreograph fashion shows in Second Life) and chemistry (you can explore virtual molecular and atomic structures by walking your avatar through them).

Still other colleges and universities have built themselves more fanciful Second Life environments. Vassar College, for example, maintains a Second Life space that is modeled to some degree on its physical brick-and-mortar presence. There are a real and a virtual Taylor Hall, Main Building, and Ferry House. The virtual Vassar space also contains an outdoor seminar area, the Seminar Swamp, along with the Vassar Amphitheater, neither of which has a real-life counterpart. On a virtual bulletin board near the Seminar Swamp, users have posted notes like, "I'm a current Vassar student and I think this is possibly the coolest thing I've ever seen. Nice job, keep up the good work!" Another has written, "This is a great island. Keep up the excellent work." Further Vassar spaces include Castle Vassar, whose rooftop garden comes complete with an open-mic stage and a wine bar.[41]

Two stunning new additions to the Vassar area are the Virtual Reality rooms. These are rooms in which the walls become a panoramic vista. Your avatar is able to turn and look in all directions as if standing on a busy Paris street or on top of a snow-capped mountain. The images are static, so the user cannot interact with the space. You cannot actually walk along the busy street, for example. But the immersive feel of the panorama would make for a great class experience as users interact with each other during the visually spectacular experience of looking out over a snowy mountain range or across a windy desert. The educational opportunity presented by this kind of visual experience is, of course, most interesting because it offers a class the opportunity to experience a location that might otherwise be inaccessible. And it is this aspect of Second Life spaces that often characterizes the best of them, such as Vassar's Sistine Chapel.

The Vassar Sistine Chapel re-creation was built by Steve Taylor, of Vassar College.[42] According to information provided in the virtual chapel, "It was built as a proof of concept, to explore how virtual reality might be used to learn about art and architecture, by experiencing the scale, context and social environment of a real-life space." So, beyond just having access to the artwork for which the Sistine Chapel is so famous, users of the space can get some sense of how that art is deployed architecturally. Of course, they can also experience the space as a social group, reacting and interacting with others in real time. And everything, we are told, is "true to scale." As such, one really does feel overwhelmed—surrounded—within the build.

Second Life experiences cannot outdo or replace their real-life equivalents (where those exist). Few people have actually made this argument, in fact, though it is commonly a straw-man position set up by those looking to argue that virtual worlds and their proponents are misguided and, as such, a bad investment for higher education. No educator who uses Second Life that I know of would ever contend that it is a substitute for real life. Arguments against Second Life that assume it becomes a refuge from and replacement for actual lives are no more useful than those that condemn the Web because online gambling is a problem for a tiny fraction of Web users. Nor might we discount a Web application like Google Maps as a replacement for reality, even though some, like Marc Horowitz and Peter Baldes, for example, have used it to replace a real-life road trip with an entirely virtual trip across the country, from L.A. to Richmond, Virginia. Horowitz and Baldes claim that "This is everything that we'd do on a real road trip, except we didn't have to leave the house, pay for gas, or worry about getting speeding tickets." Apparently, "The two friends have enjoyed their trip so far and are even planning more virtual trips. A real road trip, however, doesn't have the same appeal."[43]

In fact, Second Life experiences are often best understood and evaluated as events in and of themselves. A visit to the Sistine Chapel in Second Life, for example, can involve flying your avatar around the space. You can investigate the ceiling up close. This hardly makes the Second Life chapel experience better than a real-world visit. It is simply different. Bret Ingerman, VP for Computing and Information Services at Vassar, has commented that Vassar's investment of time and money in Second Life development has made possible a variety of experiments in teaching with immersive environments. The spaces were never designed to compete with or to replace their real-world equivalents. Many educational spaces in Second Life are not meant to recall any actual, real-life spaces at all. They are designed, rather, as social spaces, many times highlighting the degree to which Second

Life provides a platform for doing what cannot be done in real life. The space in Second Life with which I am most familiar is a good example of this: an immersive environment that brings to life William Wordsworth's famous poem, "Lines Composed a Few Miles above Tintern Abbey."[44]

Wordsworth's poem, published in 1798 as part of the collection *Lyrical Ballads*, which he produced with Samuel Coleridge, traces the poet's development as a poet, from his youth through to his more mature years. In "Tintern Abbey," Wordsworth laments the lost energy and enthusiasm of his youth but finds as recompense the more receptive poetic mind through which he can find beauty in the natural world.

What initially prompts and then enables this poetic self-reflection, though, is what Wordsworth elsewhere called a "spot of time"—the location in which the poetic reflection takes place.[45] In the case of "Tintern Abbey," the spot of time is under a sycamore tree on the banks of the River Wye, which separates England and Wales. This is a place that Wordsworth had visited a number of times throughout his life. In revisiting the spot, he is able to think about how he has changed over the many years he has been coming to the Abbey. Place thus plays a crucial role in the poem.

This made Second Life the ideal digital tool for bringing the poem to three-dimensional life. Second Life provides an immersive space in which students can explore the various natural settings that Wordsworth describes in his poem. Being in the space together, students can communicate to each other in real time their reactions and thoughts. To guide this exploration, I provide a handout (a low-tech teaching device if ever there was one) that prompts students to consider elements of the Second Life space along with excerpts from the poem and to note how or whether they feel any connection between what Wordsworth is saying and their own lives. A Journal feature allows students' responses to the prompts to be delivered directly to me.

I have used the Second Life "Tintern Abbey" in British Literature and in Composition classes with great success. Students have indicated that the immersive nature of Second Life brings the poem to life for them. The virtual space makes the poem more real for some. Students are able to see the kind of environment that Wordsworth is describing, and they are also able to better feel a part of that space.

The participatory nature of the experience even helps students to remember the poem, including Wordsworth's detailed descriptions. A former student of mine once noted, for example, "The sounds of 'waters, rolling from their mountain-springs' [a descriptive line from the poem] are still fresh in my mind having actually listened to them while reading it. The same goes for the atmosphere of the hermit's cave, or even the little picture of Dorothy Wordsworth that you guys put in there, which helps me remember that she was even mentioned in the poem, and also how important she was to William."[46]

My work with classes in Second Life has been a success, though some caveats are in order:

Second Life was just one part of a course that included other digital applications (e.g., a class discussion board), though the class also relied on much more traditional teaching tools. All students purchased the required textbook. They produced analytical essays based on the readings we were doing. And the class was fully face-to-face, not online. I took time to demonstrate and explain Second Life before we ventured in as a class. And, when we did go in-world, we were physically together in a computer lab, which made basic troubleshooting easy. I also knew that all the machines in the lab were equipped to run Second Life effectively, something on which I had worked with IT well before the semester even started.

However, faculty and students remain skeptical of applications like Second Life for two basic reasons. First, the investment of time in learning how to use the application and to set up effective learning scenarios may not, at least at first blush, seem to pay off. And, second, for some there is no clear problem that an application like Second Life overcomes. It does not seem to allow us to do anything better than we had been doing it before. Given these two factors, especially in combination, many faculty and students are not motivated to use Second Life frequently. Immersive virtual worlds remain, at least for now, a marginal activity, with some individual campuses working hard and investing heavily to develop and maintain a robust virtual presence. In other cases, individual faculty members and support personnel work to build and script in Second Life, though largely as a labor of love, not as part of an institution-wide effort to build a virtual presence. Buy-in across the higher education landscape has not yet happened. However, there are notable efforts to develop virtual learning across institutions, which reflect the direction in which higher education may be moving very soon.

For example, the University of Texas system, which includes 16 separate campuses, has made a major investment in virtual learning through its Virtual Learning Community Initiative (VLIC). According to the University of Texas system's Transforming Undergraduate Education Web site, the development of a cross-campus virtual learning space—49 islands in Second Life—is "the first of its kind in the world." The goal is to "to use 21st century technology to develop 21st century knowledge and skills."[47] Also, Texas State Technical College has, since Fall 2008, been offering a digital media certificate, the course work for which occurs primarily in Second Life. Associate degree programs in digital media or digital signage design, delivered in part via Second Life, are also available.[48] Texas Tech claims to have produced the first graduate, Julie Shannan, who obtained a degree entirely through Second Life course work; she graduated May 16, 2009.[49]

As recent history shows, technology and usage patterns change rapidly. What today is cutting edge can tomorrow become standard digital fare. So, while many remain dubious about applications like Second Life, expressing something like this student's reaction—"I believe it is a very useful tool but at the same time can be a bit scary"—it remains important for those in higher education to pursue the teaching and learning possibilities that something like Second Life provides. In this way, we can be ready when immersive environments catch on more widely.

The inevitable fact is that higher education must try more and more to engage students for whom, as Diana and James Oblinger have written, "interactivity" and "learning by doing" are paramount.[50] The standard Web tools currently in widespread use simply do not offer the same potential for immersive participation and real-time interactivity that Second Life does. The Second Life "Tintern Abbey" experience we created at College of DuPage has given my students, and others who have used the space, the opportunity to learn about a poet and a poem and to share that learning experience with one another as it unfolded, in immersive and social ways that were not previously possible.

However, with an application like Second Life, we discover, in acute form, the basic questions with which technology always confronts us: exactly what problem does it address, and how do we best use it?

So the question about whether or not Second Life is a game might be a minor issue of semantics in some cases, but, if one key to fostering broad investment within and across institutions to create and develop a Second Life presence involves increasing basic awareness, then the terms we use to talk about Second Life are crucial.

It is particularly important to understand that Second Life is not a game, inasmuch as there is no ready-made set of motivators and there is no narrative in which your avatar plays a role and because of which one event follows from another. This is not to say that there is nothing in Second Life until you build it. Of course, the opposite is true. An abundant and often busy world waits to be discovered in Second Life. Admittedly, as with the Web itself, some places in Second Life are silly, childish, or just plain boring. But, for every uninteresting virtual space there are probably two more that can provide an educational opportunity of some kind.

The key is, of course, how we use the spaces in Second Life. This is where informed curricular design becomes crucial, for, in this respect,

Second Life can become a game. As with any classroom assignment (regardless of delivery mode) it always falls to somebody (be it a professor, an individual student, a group of students, or some combination of these at various times) to establish a set of rules, or boundaries, that can contain action and drive it forward. This is the case whether or not technology is involved. For example, imagine an assignment that asks students to write an essay but provides nothing more. With no guidelines—even basic ones like minimum word count—the game of writing cannot unfold. A student given this task will surely flounder. What is the topic? Where do I start? Is this essay personal, analytical, descriptive?

Perhaps counterintuitively, we see that rules do not necessarily restrict action. Rules enable action. And, in this sense, an application like Second Life, as fancy and cutting edge as it may seem, operates best when we understand that it is not a game until somebody makes it one, that is, until, within the context of a college course, somebody establishes an objective, outlines rules and requirements for achieving that objective, and provides direction to the users whose avatars will propel the game forward.

The assumption that Second Life is, in and of itself, a game, however, is all too common. In their book *Wikinomics,* for example, Tapscott and Williams refer to Second Life directly as a "massively multiplayer online game."[51] Gloria Hillard, reporting for NPR, writes, "Want a bigger house, a svelte figure or a gender change? It's possible in the online game 'Second Life,' where residents trade real money for virtual land, designer clothes and other trappings of a fantasy life."[52] The sense that Second Life, as a game, will somehow provide, internally, the structure and impetus to make things happen is a basic misunderstanding that spirals out to create further problems. For example, Aaron Barlow, writing in *Blogging America,* argues that Second Life lacks a "'real'-world grounding."[53] Second Life does itself no favors with homepage copy like this, either: "Ready to create a new digital you?" The perceived lack of real world connection leads Barlow to speculate that "a game or experiment like Second Life" is unlikely to gain traction as widely as have other, Web-based, activities (like blogging). "One has to be someone else" in the game of Second Life, contends Barlow.[54]

However, Second Life is not a game. At most, it might be a game waiting to happen, a setting that needs assignment-specific rules, guidelines, and objectives to be established by the community that has agreed to play (which might include a class or a group of students). Once these constraints are in place, there is no necessity to be someone else, or to role-play, as one might have to in a true massively multiuser online role playing game.

Barlow's ultimate concern is an important one, though. In *Blogging America*, for example, at issue is the potential for weblogs to (re)invent a 21st-century public sphere. The subtitle of Barlow's book is, after all, *The New Public Sphere.* Understanding Second Life as removed from a public reality thus leads Barlow to undervalue its potential. But, if we actually see immersive environments like Second Life as the setting for a public sphere waiting to happen, we go a long way to getting at the potential for Second Life to be an important 21st-century learning tool, not just another game in which players act out roles within a fantastical, preexisting narrative that is largely prescriptive and removed from a public reality of any kind.

Indeed, the point of playing a game in the most conventional sense is to escape from the real public sphere for a short time. This is perhaps why the name of the platform, Second Life, connotes everything that is problematic about technology for so many who are not actively involved with it. A second life suggests removal from, or an alternative to, a first life. The distinction between the virtual and the real—as entirely separate lives—is precisely what most games aim to provide, but this is exactly what Second Life, as an educational tool, does not necessarily need to become. Avatars can look as otherworldly as users prefer, and the spaces avatars inhabit can be strange and fantastic. But the social interaction—the linguistic maneuvering in a communal space—is quite real.

One anecdote is instructive in this regard. A colleague of mine tells the story of using Second Life for a portion of a class for English majors in rhetoric and discourse.[55] The focus for the class was how language is and can be used in different circumstances. The professor notes that students "liked the idea of creating an alternative identity and expressing that identity in different visual forms." This is the game or role play aspect that Second Life provides, the escape from First Life. But creating and outfitting an avatar was only the beginning. Second Life became particularly useful in the rhetoric and discourse class as a venue that the professor "could use in class to generate a piece of discourse which could then be immediately examined." In other words, the real interaction of people represented virtually took primacy.

The useful teaching moment came when, as my colleague describes, "I went into the grid with my avatar and started up a conversation with a woman who turned out to be a Second Life dancer. When the conversation started to get raunchy, I bailed, but we were left with a pretty rich dialogue which led to some terrific analysis." The virtual world provided a platform for real linguistic exchange that would have otherwise been very difficult, if not impossible, for the class to experience. The broader point is that Second Life can provide a real public sphere of discourse, even if that sphere is for the most part limited to a single group of students, as opposed to providing an escape from the real public sphere. As Tom Funk argues, "online social networks have become, for many, the new public square."[56] Second Life just happens to provide a fully immersive social—or public sphere—experience, unlike the Web, which preserves a much more obvious sense of mediation between the user and his or her digital world.

Philip Rosedale, the founder and chief executive of Linden Labs, the company that operates the Second Life platform, has argued that "Second Life competes in many ways with the real world, offering better ways to collaborate, meet people, and build things."[57] But the language of citizenship is equally important in Rosedale's view. What we can learn through using Second Life, he argues, is not just a set of technical skills (whether it is basic avatar movement, communicating, building, or scripting); rather, Rosedale says, "As every free society has discovered, we have realized, more and more over time, how much our community [in Second Life] is a developing nation."[58]

Where Aaron Barlow sees Second Life as a game-based utility, removed from the important (re)emerging public sphere of the 21st century that is being enabled by online applications like blogs, Rosedale argues the opposite, seeing instead the space of Second Life as a virtual setting for the real creation and exploration of social interactions and dynamics. In using Second Life as an effective educational technology within the blended or hybrid environment it is vital to understand that the platform itself does not, as a technology, provide a removed, fantastical narrative—a game—in which users can pretend to be something that they are not.

Second Life is immediately attractive for many because it is filled with interesting spaces to explore. In an afternoon, I toured the North Carolina State Wolflands, the NC State Second Life campus that features gathering spaces, library services, vending machines…everything you might find on a real campus. I also visited the Virtual Stomach Museum and then the National Oceanic and Atmospheric Administration's Second Life space, where I rode a weather balloon into the eye of a hurricane. I next visited a virtual Mendel's garden and learned about the principle of independent assortment. From the garden, I headed to the Biomedicine Research Organization and swam around inside a larger-than-life eukaryotic cell.

To be sure, there is no shortage of places and objects in Second Life. I even took an underwater tour, complete with killer whales, leaping dolphins, and an octopus. But the abundance of things and places to explore in Second Life, while initially attractive to many, is not likely to generate a critical mass of interested educators, administrators, or students.

What matters is not the stuff in Second Life but the social interaction that is possible as groups visit and experience that stuff together.

In this sense, Second Life is little different from a much more common and culturally visible application like Facebook. Most students do not use Facebook because they can add a lot of neat or unusual widgets to their Facebook pages. They use it, as common sense tells us, for its social aspect. Educators would do well to understand and approach Second Life, and other kinds of newer technologies like it, not for the content it provides (though this can be exciting, as in the Sistine Chapel example) but for the kind of socially interactive opportunities it provides. Higher education is more and more prizing collaborative knowledge building, and Second Life can provide the real feeling of having been some place and of having experienced something, though virtually, with somebody else.

Even more than just having students visit a Web site and then share their individual experiences after the fact, Second Life allows groups of students to inhabit and explore a virtual space together in real time and to share their reactions synchronously as the experience unfolds. The sense that Second Life provides of having done something as a class, even when the physical members of that class are not actually together, is by far the most promising aspect of virtual worlds.

In this regard, it is crucial to understand the way in which an immersive environment, a virtual world, mediates an experience differently than does the traditional 2-D Web. Where, in using the Web, the physical me looks at a screen, in a virtual world we have the addition of a virtual me. So, as the user, I actually have the experience of watching my virtual self move through a space and interact with others. Rather than producing a distancing effect, as though I were now twice removed from an experience (the real me sees the virtual me see something), users often find the opposite to be true. Second Life produces a greater sense of presence or immediacy as one has the feeling of actually being within a built environment, sitting on a chair, gesturing, and moving physically from one group conversation to another.

Joanne Martin, president of IBM's prestigious Academy of Technology, had this to say about the virtual conference that the Academy hosted in Second Life: "The immersion resulted in a very strange psychological effect, where part of me really felt like I was physically there. And I would watch myself walk around and talk to people." And Craig Becker, lead architect/designer for the IBM virtual conference meeting spaces, commented that "When people woke up the morning after the virtual meetings and thought about the day before, it wasn't like remembering a webcast or a phone conference. We truly felt as if we had attended a real-time meeting."[59]

In fact, a skill that may become more and more valuable, perhaps even essential, in the global workplace is the ability to navigate and to communicate effectively in immersive environments like Second Life. The student of today may tomorrow become the professional whose avatar is responsible for creating and delivering presentations to clients who are physically distributed across the globe but who have gathered together virtually in a digital meeting space. As Steve Mills of IBM has noted, "When computers run fast enough, and the bandwidth is there, everything that is remote feels local. . . . I don't need to be present in the room to participate."[60]

In fact, in 2008, IBM's Academy of Technology held both its virtual conference and an annual meeting in Second Life. The Second Life space included areas for keynote presentations and breakout sessions, along with a library and various areas for community gathering. Academy president Joanne Martin noted that "The meeting in Second Life was everything that you could do at a traditional conference—and more—at one fifth the cost and without a single case of jet lag."[61]

Diane Berry, CEO of Trade Promotion Management Associates, said of their first in-world conference, which occurred in February 2009, "I was also pleasantly surprised that, just as you have in a live meeting, at the end of our sessions we had people lingering in groups, chatting together. Our organizations foster collaboration between retailers and suppliers; this was highly valuable because it was highly collaborative."[62] The meeting involved some 160 participants from a variety of international commercial, retail, and industry groups. Both flexible and cost-effective, immersive environments may become more and more the collaborative norm. As such, effective communication in a mediated environment like Second Life may indeed become a core 21st-century workplace skill.

EXIT REALITY: THE SOCIAL WEB

The Second Life Web site provides useful data on user log-ins and user transactions. Over the course of a typical week, for example, about 60,000 users are reported to have logged in. Second Life also indicates that its user base is well over one million people. The numbers are substantial—and growing—but it may still be a while before we see the kind of broad public participation that it would take to make Second Life a standard feature in higher education. Even the Web, which is otherwise culturally ubiquitous, is still not necessarily a feature in every college and university class.

One interesting trend that brings the social element of Second Life to the Web browser interfaces with which so many people are already familiar involves 3-D Web technology as is available from Exit Reality.[63] Users download a Web browser plug-in that operates within the browser they already use, like Firefox or Internet Explorer. The plug-in renders standard Web pages as 3-D, immersive spaces. They often look like the virtual worlds of Second Life. And you are represented by a digital avatar (though this feature can be turned off if you find it distracting). Instead of browsing a 2-D Web page as you normally would, your avatar moves through a Web space rendered in three dimensions.

The system is not terribly useful if you are using the Web to find information, especially from a Web site that does not maintain a dedicated 3-D presence, because of the way that Exit Reality renders the visual field. When I used Exit Reality to visit my college's homepage in 3-D to look up registration information, for example, my avatar found himself among large billboards (images from the 2-D Web site) and numerous clickable flagposts (links from the 2-D Web site). The visual field was not very user friendly. You cannot, for example, see very many links at one time. And text is rendered poorly if at all, sometimes appearing on the floor of the 3-D space. Some have argued that "nobody hangs around in the 'publish and browse' Internet anymore,"[64] but this is not always the case. Sometimes the real me just needs basic information.

But visit a site that has been designed to exist in a 3-D space, and the results can be quite different. As part of the Exit Reality plaza, for example (which is where your avatar finds itself when you launch the application), you can find 3-D Hardees and Carl's Jr. restaurants (both owned by CKE Restaurants, Inc.). In press material for the launch of the 3-D restaurants and for CKE's partnership with Exit Reality, Brad Haley, executive vice president of marketing for Carl's Jr. and Hardees, explains that "We've always tried to stay on the cutting-edge when it comes to the development of our new burgers and advertising, so it made sense for us to associate ourselves with cutting-edge technologies in the digital world as well."[65]

I also checked out Facebook as it exists in a 3-D Exit Reality version. I walked my avatar into the Facebook building, through the front doors, and into my virtual apartment—my own Facebook page realized in 3-D. Were I inclined, I could get virtual take-out from one of the burger joints and enjoy, if not an actual meal, then at least the bag and cup sitting on my virtual apartment desk.

But I am not inclined to do that. There is really not much going on in the Exit Reality space, including the restaurants or the Warner Brothers movie theater I walked into, which was mostly 3-D advertising and retail. As Haley's comments in connection with Hardees and Carl's

Jr.'s presence in the 3-D environment suggest, it is right now all about a brand presence in a space that might, in the future, appeal to the younger market that the real-world restaurants believe they serve. In Haley's terms, "Our brands cater to young, hungry guys and gals in the real world and this cool new software from ExitReality will allow them to experience the Web in a way they've never been able to before, so we were thrilled to be able to help present that to them."[66]

But what begins as an exercise in marketing and brand penetration could easily become the next Web trend, even though we have yet to see broad user buy-in at this point. Facebook went from an online tool for Harvard students in 2004 to a social Web site with an international user base of some 200 million just five years later. If users get past the overt commercialism of the 3-D Web (at least as it has been rolled out by Exit Reality) and catch on to its potential as an immersive social space, it may indeed become the next seemingly overnight success story. Clearly Hardees and Carl's Jr. are hoping so.

AND NOW, THE NEXT BIG THING...

If only it were a matter of gazing into the crystal ball and pronouncing what next big thing is on the horizon! The best we can do is to identify trends and make educated guesses based on those trends. What will most certainly mark the next big thing to catch on for Web users generally, and what will most likely characterize emerging trends in higher education technology use, is that digital applications will enable collaboration and a social experience even when participants are geographically dispersed. We see the ability to operate in a virtual world like Second Life becoming a more and more visible and valuable asset for organizations, some of which are already reaping the benefits from virtually enabled collaboration. Virtual collaboration, in other words, is producing real results.

From a pedagogical perspective within higher education, though, an important element we see in looking at all of these various technologies is that each allows for a kind of meta-analysis. In fact, technology may work most productively as a learning tool not just when we are using it but when we are reflecting on exactly how and why we are using it. In other words, what is often most promising from an educational point of view is that, in building a wiki or working collaboratively in Second Life, we do not just produce some digital artifact, engage with virtual content, or learn a basic technical skill. Rather, in working virtually, we experience the real dynamics of collaboration. We see how language is used to shape and share an experience. And we can begin to understand broader social forces and pressures that govern group dynamics, both large and small. Again, why does that wiki not become a mess of vandalism and misinformation?

As Bret Ingerman has noted, Vassar College's investment in Second Life has paid off in indirect ways. He says, for example, that the institution's work in the virtual environment has served "as a catalyst for discussions here at Vassar on the role of virtual worlds." Ingerman goes on, "Our work on our islands has also served as a place where other educators have been able to see what might be possible.... The Sistine Chapel is successful on many fronts, not the least of which is drawing attention to whether or not such recreations are a valuable adjunct to visiting a location in the real world."[67]

What Ingerman's comments reveal is that technology use can become the catalyst for broader questioning and debate. Too often, both individuals and institutions may feel that these questions and debates need to be settled before investment in technology can happen. But when questions, even outright skepticism, are intentionally made a part of technology use in higher education, we can reap benefits far beyond just the teaching of basic content or skills sets with a new digital tool. The very mode of that content's delivery can become subject for discussion and debate.

Finally, the various technologies discussed here can ultimately help to create within a class a sense of communal experience and to foster in individuals the sense that they are contributing to a public sphere of dialogue, debate, knowledge, and ideas. Technology, be it relatively conventional or leading edge, does not have to figure in learning experiences in higher education. In fact, as Tom Funk writes of technology and business, "the key to participating as a company is first to participate as a person."[68] This is equally good advice for educators: it makes sense to first participate as an everyday user before working with technology in your role as an educator.

With learning objectives and workplace realities changing as we move into the 21st century, technology becomes a more and more obvious educational tool to help us achieve greater student engagement and to realize a broader vision of what learning can be.

CHAPTER 7

A Resistant Early Adopter Argues for Hybridity

In his introduction to *Digital Diploma Mills,* author David Noble paints a rather bleak picture of what e-learning might look like in the future: "young people with a background like mine—that is, without means—will not be welcomed to the campus and into the community...for a genuine education, but will be told instead to go online for training, and to do it all alone."[1] Of course, this is one possibility: education becomes a program of self-directed and self-paced study, with little or no guidance from knowledgeable faculty and with little or no interaction among students. This seems to have been at least one path that distance education has followed almost from its very inception. However, technology—the online part of the equation—is not necessarily to blame, for Noble's vision of an isolated education that amounts to little more than training could (and unfortunately does) occur in entirely face-to-face classrooms across the nation.

Noble assumes that computer-mediated communication is always cold or impersonal. Many students—and many faculty—might like to differ. As one student commented, during a North Carolina State Graduate School colloquium, for example, "My parents don't understand. They think that talking online must be impersonal. Or that it leaves some sort of void. Online is how I talk. I can communicate with so many more people and manage so many more relationships. She [her mother] thinks I'm more isolated than her generation—I think it's the opposite."[2]

Noble is right about one thing, however. The primary issue that educators face as we move into the 21st century is how to engage students, be it online or face-to-face or in a blend of these two environments. To say that hybrid courses may offer the best of both worlds has become, already, a tired cliché, though there may be some truth to it. Undeniably, hybrid courses provide educators with a broadened array of tools with which to engage students in meaningful learning.

Too often we hear complaints from dissatisfied faculty about the lack of interest or engagement shown by students. And we are even asked to believe that the generation of students under 30, born in the age of the Internet, is, as Mark Bauerlein has called them, "the dumbest generation."[3]

This should be offensive to those under 30, though most of them (if we believe Bauerlein and his adherents) are unlikely to read his book, anyway. Faculty who teach these students may feel equally offended, sensing perhaps that they have played a part in stupefying the Net generation. Certainly, many teachers have looked out at a classroom of faces, hoping to see a glimmer of interest and intellectual curiosity rather than the glazed sag of the disinterested educational customer. So take or leave Bauerlein's assertion that one generation is, or could be, dumber than another, whatever that means exactly; it is hard to ignore the demands on faculty to engage students in meaningful ways. Blended courses do not solve the problem, but they do provide a broad host of possibilities, and hybrid learning as an educational model provides faculty with an ideal setting for re-envisioning teaching from the ground up.

Gerald Graff, in his Fall 2008 President's Column in the *Modern Language Association Newsletter*, provides a rather more productive reading of the problem that Bauerlein identifies. Graff first notes just how typical have been faculty complaints about student investment and engagement for the past century. Complaints by faculty about students' vacant stares are hardly new. The real problem now, however, is not whether students can learn and retain (or want to learn and retain) information (which seems to be the barometer by which Bauerlein measures dumbness) but rather how such information can be situated in meaningful contexts that allow students to truly feel engaged, invested, and part of the debate at hand.

In other words, what we need is a greater breadth of tools to allow students to collaborate with each other, build knowledge together, and dispute and defend viewpoints in a public forum. Basic content needs to be contextualized as part of a considered intellectual position. As Graff notes, "When no such arguments are at hand, we drown in the information overload of the media and now the Internet."[4] So, while our information-laden cultural landscape would seem to be the ideal breeding ground for better informed citizens, we find that the opposite is the case: information is so plentiful that it ceases to make any sense, to possess any shape, or to have any relevance outside of itself. Graff writes, "unless information is tied to issues we care about, we retain it only superficially or not at all." He further cites Christopher Lasch, who argued, in 1990, that "what democracy requires is public debate, not information." And, "since the public no longer participates in debates on national issues, it has no reason to be better informed."[5]

Here is the ideal opening for blending the collaborative opportunities offered by online learning with the community and relationship building opportunities offered by face-to-face learning.

The varied opportunities to participate that are enabled by the hybrid model will, ideally, produce students who see the value in, well, paying attention. Almost any class can become the setting in which participants are invested in the creation of a public sphere, an arena for productive discussion, dialogue, and even disagreement.

THE END?

In fact, we find ourselves at a beginning, an exciting moment in higher education during which we may be witnessing the initial stages in blended learning's becoming the next wave in curricular design and delivery. Many students today must take an online class as part of completing a degree. Blended learning may take on this kind of institutional visibility and value in the near future, and hybrids may become as common a part of the higher education landscape as have traditional face-to-face and fully online classes.

So we are at a moment when broad and clear thinking about the implications and assumptions that surround blended learning is crucial. Individual faculty members have been making choices about teaching with technology for years. But the constituencies that have a stake in organized blended learning are growing. To argue effectively for course design and delivery that put students first, faculty, administrators, and student support staff across institutions need to be informed and able to see the broad implications of local decision making.

We are also undoubtedly at a moment when pressures on higher education are acute, regardless of the type or size of the school we are talking about. Colleges and universities are facing problems as fundamental as insufficient classroom space and limited parking for commuting students. Institutions are working hard to manage enrollment, balance budgets, strengthen student retention, improve success, and deepen engagement.

Blended learning presents an exciting opportunity to address these problems. But it is not a single solution. It may even appear to be too obvious a direction for some institutions: offer more hybrid classes and the classroom space problem is solved!! As we have seen, it is not that easy. Hybrid learning is just one promising piece of a much larger puzzle.

Many institutions are in the midst of re-imagining themselves so that they can effectively meet the 21st-century challenges of preparing students for a rapidly changing global world in which local action and awareness are becoming more and more crucial.

Knowledgeable and informed discussion will be an absolute must if blended learning is to flourish as a truly innovative opportunity for teaching and learning.

At a Glance: What It Takes to Make Hybrid Learning Work

The caveat to each of the profiles that follow is that while we may attempt to identify trends or outline some general principles, there will always be exceptions to the rule. Local contingencies and contexts trump a one-size-fits-all approach. Indeed, what we ultimately see as most promising about hybrid learning is its potential to be effective, even though it may take many forms:

Student Profile: What institutions need to consider in terms of blended course design and delivery while keeping the student in mind

- The student population taking hybrid classes is not necessarily a homogeneous group. Many could be adult students with full-time career and family obligations. Just as many could be students coming directly out of high school with a real interest in technology. Efforts to understand who is taking hybrid courses can help in tailoring classes so that they are as effective as possible.

- Some students, even despite the best of institutional efforts, will arrive to class without understanding that they have enrolled in a blended or hybrid course. Faculty should understand what this will mean for first-day introductions...and explanations.

- Many students will assume that "more flexible" (the rhetoric often attached to blended course offerings) means "less work."

- Technology may be identified by students as the root cause of their poor performance if they do not succeed academically. Technology may thus appear to have a consistently negative effect on retention. However, technology is less often the actual cause of poor academic performance than qualitative or casual student reporting would indicate. Technology is just an easy scapegoat when a more honest reckoning of poor performance would identify basic problems of too little time on task, too little investment in course work, and ineffective, or nonexistent, time management.

- Students who are already at academic risk or who already have full schedules may gravitate to alternative delivery models because these modes are advertised as flexible. Students looking for maximum flexibility may be juggling too many responsibilities to be successful in any delivery format. The student population taking hybrid classes may very well represent a group that is already likely to under perform, because they have sought out a delivery mode that provides them with an additional class where one should not really fit. This is even more true for online learning populations.

- So-called tech-savvy or Net generation students are not necessarily more likely to be successful than other students in online or hybrid courses; they may, in fact, approach technology in a manner exactly the opposite of what they need in order to be successful in an educational setting.

- For many students (of all ages), technology in their everyday lives means ease and convenience, so part of hybrid learning may involve helping students to learn to approach technology differently.

Course Profile: What a successful hybrid course might look like and what it will require

- Hybrids usually require focused, face-to-face technical orientation on the first day of class.

- Well-coordinated f2f and online components, each tied to clear learning objectives, will help students to feel that they are taking one class, not two.

- A clear, week-by-week course schedule that makes the relationship of online and f2f time transparent will help students (and faculty) to stay on track.

- Technology should meet a well-defined need that is made transparent to students.

- Activities should take place in the mode to which they are best suited.
    - F2f for energetic discussion, student presentations, and the introduction of complex concepts/topics
    - Online for regularly recurring time for reflection, substantial writing, repeatable self-assessment

- Technology need not be complex to serve pedagogical purposes effectively.

- Equally successful blended courses may look entirely different from one another, so there is no recipe to guarantee success.

Institutional Obligations: What institutions that push for increased hybrid offerings should consider as part of supporting successful teaching and learning experiences

- Because not all institutions are the same, following an existing, even a proven, model for organizing resources related to blended learning will not necessarily reproduce results achieved in other contexts.

- Highly visible, even intrusive, disclaimers should accompany all hybrid course advertising; this language should state, as clearly as possible, that hybrid courses involve technology, that they meet for less time but often involve more work than their f2f counterparts, and that hybrids are not self-paced or independent learning modes.

- Ample course design education for faculty should be made available (this needs to be flexible and repeated on a regular basis).

- Accommodation should be provided to allow for the development of a faculty community—online and f2f—for those teaching or thinking about teaching hybrids; it is especially important that there be an opportunity for faculty to share best practices across disciplines; a blended learning wiki within or across departments is ideal for this.

- Investment in hardware and software for faculty (for use at home and on campus), without excessive administrative paperwork or other barriers to adoption, can foster innovation and can make teaching in the hybrid mode more attractive to many faculty.

- Course release time to allow faculty to develop new hybrid courses, to improve or revise courses, and to re-educate themselves on a regular basis (not just once to support the initial creation of a hybrid course) will help to ensure quality blended course offerings.

- IT support should be available for students regardless of whether online/hybrid classes are using course management software or external applications (e.g., wikis, blogs).

- IT support needs to be available for students and staff during extended hours, seven days per week.

- Administrators must understand that faculty (and students) gravitate to hybrid teaching and learning for a variety of reasons, not necessarily because of a pre-existing interest in (or facility with) technology; thus, mixed-mode curricular design and teaching will not be a labor of love for most faculty members to which they can be expected to devote substantial personal time.

- Online support services for students (e.g., library and advising help) must be accessible and highly visible; students can take advantage of great resources only when those resources can be found.

- Administrators must be aware that increased blended offerings will not, de facto, alleviate problems of physical classroom space and that administrative mandates about the structure of individual hybrids (e.g., Faculty member X must divide time 50/50 and must teach on Tuesday/Thursday, with Thursday as the face-to-face day) will likely meet with considerable faculty resistance.

Faculty Obligations: What faculty who express an interest in designing and teaching hybrid courses should be prepared to take on as attendant responsibilities, recognizing the necessary and ongoing time commitment. Faculty will have to

- Actively pursue formal and/or informal professional development related to teaching with technology and effective instructional design.

- Devote appropriate face-to-face classroom time to orienting students to technology to help students feel more at ease in the blended environment. Faculty should be aware of how this student support will affect time in class that is available for content coverage.

- Provide extra, out-of-class technical assistance to blended learning students (these students will likely turn to the class professor before turning to institutional IT support); this instructor-based IT support role will continue past the initial orientation days in class.

- Commit to assessing hybrid course outcomes relative to outcomes in other delivery modes (outcomes include, broadly, student success and retention).

- Identify if or where technology per se is presenting a barrier to student success.

- Solicit student feedback specifically on the hybrid delivery mode and revise curricula accordingly.

- Make efforts to develop a community of those designing and teaching hybrid classes, which will require individual faculty time and commitment, because such a community is vital to fostering the exchange of best practices across an institution.

Notes

INTRODUCTION

1. Ken King, "Foreword," *Transforming Teaching with Technology: Perspectives from Two-Year Colleges,* ed. Kamala Anandam (McKinney, TX: Academic Computing Publications), xiv.

2. Sir John Daniel, "Lessons from the Open University: Low-Tech Learning Often Works Best," *Chronicle of Higher Education,* September 7, 2001, http://chronicle.com/weekly/v48/i02/02b02401.htm.

3. One university professor, published and well known in the field of blended learning, actually noted to me in an e-mail: "Although I remain an advocate for BL [blended learning], my research activities in this area have declined largely because our institution went through a leadership change and this focus was lost to a certain degree."

4. Anthony G. Picciano and Charles D. Dziuban, *Blended Learning: Research Perspectives* (Needham, MA: Sloan Consortium, 2007).

5. The phrase "resistance is futile" has even earned itself a Wikipedia entry: http://en.wikipedia.org/wiki/Resistance_is_futile.

6. See "Umass Online," Tech Support and Requirements, UMass Online, http://www.umassonline.net/TechSupport.html. And see "Evening Hybrid Program," Sandhills Community College, http://www.sandhills.edu/usp/hybrid.html.

7. Because the idea of hybridity is right now so culturally prevalent and so charged, there may not be a case in which the language of "the hybrid" does not obviously connote either positive or negative value. In other words, the value-neutral hybrid may not, because discursively it cannot, exist.

8. Find these at KEEN's homepage, http://www.keenfootwear.com./.

9. Beth Hewett, "Re: Survey about Hybrid/Online First-Year Writing Courses," WPA listserv, March 24, 2008, https://lists.asu.edu/cgi-bin/wa?A2= ind0803&L=WPA-L&T=0&F=&S=&P=69495.

10. Beth Hewett, e-mail correspondence with the author, April 23, 2009.

11. Margie Martyn, "The Online Blended Model," *Educause Quarterly*, no. 1 (2003): 18–23.

12. Catherine Gouge, "Conversation at a Crucial Moment: Hybrid Courses and the Future of Writing Programs," *College English* 71, no. 4 (March 2009), 338–362.

13. "What Term Does Your Institution Use?" *Sloan-C Blended Learning*, http://www.blendedteaching.org/.

CHAPTER 1: THE RESISTANT EARLY ADOPTER

1. Todd Gitlin, *Media Unlimited: How the Torrent of Images and Sounds Overwhelms Our Lives* (New York: Metropolitan Books, 2001).

2. Among the many interesting books that address problems of technology and education, see Todd Oppenheimer, *The Flickering Mind: Saving Education from the False Promise of Technology* (New York: Random House, 2003); Larry Cuban, *Teachers and Machines: The Classroom Use of Technology since 1920* (New York: Teachers College Press, 1986); and Tara Brabazon, *The University of Google* (Burlington, VT: Ashgate, 2007).

3. Mark Bauerlein, "Turned On, Plugged In, Online, & Dumb: Student Failure Despite the Techno Revolution," *Encyclopedia Britannica* blog, October 21, 2008. http://www.britannica.com/blogs/2008/10/turned-on-plugged-in-online-dumb-student-failure-despite-the-techno-revolution.

4. Robert Reid, "Effective E-Learning? Not by a Long Chalk," *RobertReid. Edublogs*, October 21, 2008, http://robertreid.edublogs.org/2008/10/21/ effective-e-learning-not-by-a-long-chalk.

5. "Greater Expectations: A New Vision for Learning as a Nation Goes to College," *Association of American Colleges and Universities*, 2002, http://www. greaterexpectations.org/.

6. Van B. Weigel, *Deep Learning for a Digital Age: Technology's Untapped Potential to Enrich Higher Education* (San Francisco: Jossey Bass, 2002), xiii.

CHAPTER 2: CHALLENGES FACING HIGHER EDUCATION

1. The College of DuPage homepage is http://www.cod.edu.

2. "College of DuPage Institutional Priorities, January 5–June 20, 2009," Office of the President, College of DuPage, January, 2009.

3. I will point out again that I am not attempting to single out my home institution as unique or unusual in this example. I choose COD as the example because I have access to the internal communication, the "Institutional

Priorities" circulated by the president's office, that would not otherwise be available.

4. "College of DuPage Institutional Priorities."

5. "COD Online Course Delivery Survey Fall 08," College of DuPage, January 2009. Respondents could choose from among these response options: "classroom section was closed"; "classroom section was scheduled at inconvenient times"; "fit with personal learning style." Alternately, respondents could supply their own reason for choosing the online delivery mode.

6. "Institutional Priorities 2007–2008," College of DuPage Mission and Priorities, College of DuPage, August 26, 2008, http://www.cod.edu/mission_priorities/priorities.htm.

7. "COD Officially Announces New President," *Daily Herald,* November 12, 2008, http://www.dailyherald.com/story/?id=249986.

8. Institutional rhetoric about growth is hardly limited to two-year institutions. For example, Rice University's "A Vision for Rice University's 2nd Century" includes this mandate: "We must increase the size of the university to realize more fully our ambition as an institution of national and international distinction that attracts the very best students and researchers from around the globe" (http://www.professor.rice.edu/professor/Vision.asp).

9. Such phrases, or ones that are very similar, can be discovered in print advertising and on innumerable college Web pages.

10. The COD Student Portrait for Fall 2007 indicates that total seat count falls primarily in the "morning," rather than in the "afternoon" or "evening"; more than 40 percent of students registered for morning classes, whereas the afternoon and evening drew 23 percent and 25 percent, respectively. Another 10 percent of respondents reported "TBA/Unknown." See "Student Portrait, Fall Semester 2007," Office of Research and Planning, College of DuPage, November 2007, 15.

11. "Institutional Portrait, 2007–2008," Office of Research and Planning, College of DuPage, October 2007, 38. Enrollment at the College of DuPage was reported in Fall 2006 at 26,032, making it the fourth largest single-campus two-year college in the nation.

12. It is important to note that enrollment count comparisons—and thus determination of a "largest" school—can be difficult because enrollment numbers can be computed in many different ways. How, or if, schools adjust for part-time versus full-time enrollment, for example, can affect enrollment reporting.

13. Jeffrey R. Young, "'Hybrid' Teaching Seeks to End the Divide between Traditional and Online Instruction," *Chronicle of Higher Education,* March 22, 2002, http://chronicle.com/free/v48/i28/28a03301.htm.

14. See http://www.mtsac.edu/about/mission.html and http://www.palomar.edu/goals.htm.

15. "Liberal Education and America's Promise (LEAP)," Association of American Colleges and Universities, http://www.aacu.org/leap/vision.cfm.

16. "Essential Learning Outcomes," Association of American Colleges and Universities, http://www.aacu.org/leap/vision.cfm.

17. Catherine Stover, "Measuring—and Understanding—Student Retention," *Distance Education Report* 9, no. 16 (August 15, 2005): 1.

18. See "2009 Retention/Completion Summary Tables," ACT, http://www.act.org/research/policymakers/pdf/09retain_trends.pdf.

19. Ormond Simpson, *Student Retention in Online, Open and Distance Learning* (Sterling, VA: Kogan Page, 2003), 2.

20. "National Collegiate Retention and Persistence to Degree Rates," ACT, 2008.

21. It is worth recognizing that not all students enrolled at two-year schools plan to complete a degree at all. In fact, the Student Portrait Fall Semester 2007 for the College of DuPage indicates that only 55 percent of students answered yes to the question, "Do you plan to graduate from C.O.D.?" (30).

22. Ibid., 6.

23. M. Lee Upcraft, "Foreword," *Connecting to the Net Generation* (National Association of Student Personnel Administrators, 2007), xii.

24. Updates to Twitter pages, or "streams," are called "tweets."

25. Diana G. Oblinger, "Growing Up with Google: What It Means to Education," *Emerging Technologies for Learning* 3 (March 2008): 11.

26. "Plane Crash Survivor Texts Twitter Updates," Guardian.co.uk, December 22, 2008, http://www.guardian.co.uk/world/blog/2008/dec/22/plane-crash-twitter.

27. A follower is somebody who has signed up to be notified every time a Twitter stream is updated, which, in some cases, is often.

28. Facebook users can find the Pizza Hut page by using the Facebook search box.

29. "TiVo To Help Couch Potatoes Get Pizza," NPR Morning Edition, November 18, 2008, http://www.npr.org/templates/story/story.php?storyId=97124780.

30. "Teens, Video Games, and Civics," Pew Internet and American Life Project, September 2008, http://www.pewinternet.org/Reports/2008/Teens-Video-Games-and-Civics.aspx, 1.

31. These are also sometimes referred to as Learning Management Systems (LMS).

32. Oblinger, "Growing Up with Google," 11.

33. See http://twitter.com. Text on the Twitter homepage changes frequently, though it invariably stresses the idea that users "connect," "share," and "discover" by using Twitter.

34. This particular user goes by the name, AFineFrenzy. Her Twitter stream is at http://twitter.com/AFineFrenzy.

35. "Watch What You Tweet," *Democracy Now,* October 7, 2009, http://www.democracynow.org/blog/2009/10/7/watch_what_you_tweet.

36. Oblinger, "Growing Up with Google,"15.

37. Carie Windham, "The Student's Perspective," *Educating the Net Generation* (Educause, 2005), http://www.educause.edu/Resources/Educatingth eNetGeneration/TheStudentsPerspective/6061. Windham was, at the time of her contribution to *Educating the Net Generation,* a history major at North Carolina State University.

38. IMing, or instant messaging, is synchronous, text-based communication that can happen via computer or mobile phone/PDA. IM and "chat" generally refer to the same thing, where "chat" is also a text-based activity. "Texting" is related, though it does not necessarily happen synchronously. A "text" can be sent from one user to another (via cell phone, for example), and the recipient may respond immediately or, as is the case with e-mail, at a later time. Regardless, texting usually involves all kinds of "unconventional" spelling, grammar, and formatting. Anybody who has texted using a cell phone realizes that these unconventional choices are the product of having to "type" a message using limited keys and not necessarily evidence of poor writing skills.

39. "Writing, Technology, and Teens," Pew Internet and American Life Project, April 24, 2008, http://www.pewinternet.org/Reports/2008/Writing-Technology-and-Teens.aspx, v.

40. Quoted in Sam Dillon, "What Corporate America Cannot Build: A Sentence," New York Times, December 7, 2004, http://query.nytimes.com/gst/fullpage.html?res=9B05EFDB1531F934A35751C1A9629C8B63.

41. Quoted in Markus Berkmann, "TXTING: THE GR8 DB8," New York Post, July 27, 2008, http://www.nypost.com/p/news/opinion/books/txtng_the_gr_db_4pSUZstfEH2aFkdsqLBEEK.

42. Quoted in Dillon, "What Corporate America Cannot Build."

43. "Writing, Technology, and Teens," 3.

44. Find "Imagining the Internet: A History and Forecast" at http://www.imaginingtheinternet.org/. This is a project co-sponsored by the Pew Internet and American Life Project and Elon University.

45. "Imagining the Internet: A History and Forecast," http://www.elon.edu/e-web/predictions/metaverse/book_transcript.xhtml.

46. "The Horizon Report, 2008 Edition," New Media Consortium and the Educause Learning Initiative, http://www.nmc.org/pdf/2008-Horizon-Report.pdf, 7.

47. "Generations Online," Pew Internet and American Life Project, December 2005, http://www.pewinternet.org/pdfs/PIP_Generations_Memo.pdf.

48. The Pew Internet and American Life Project has studied the digital divide extensively. See http://www.pewinternet.org/topics/digital-divide.aspx. While the concept of the digital divide has a long history, the term itself gained currency in the mid-1990s.

49. I have known students who, for example, drive to campus to use the open computer lab to complete work for an online class.

50. "Technical Readiness," COD Online, http://www.cod.edu/Online/technical.htm.

51. "Profiles of Successful Online Students," Illinois Board of Higher Education, http://www.ibhe.state.il.us/consumerinfo/elearning.htm.

52. The College of DuPage "Software and Hardware Recommendations" page suggests that students' minimum Internet connection speed be "56 kbps Dial-up Modem." The "recommended" Internet connection is "Any high-speed connection (e.g. Cable Broadband or DSL)."

53. "Umass Online," Tech Support and Requirements, http://www.umassonline.net/TechSupport.html.

54. "Rural Broadband Internet Use," Pew Internet and American Life Project, Data memo, February 2006, http://www.pewinternet.org/~/media/Files/Reports/2006/PIP_Rural_Broadband.pdf.pdf.

55. "Home Broadband Adoption 2008," Pew Internet and American Life Project, July 2008, http://www.pewinternet.org/pdfs/PIP_Broadband_2008.pdf, ii.

56. "Broadband Growth and Policies in OECD Countries." Organization for Economic Cooperation and Development, prepublication version, June 2008, http://www.oecd.org/dataoecd/32/57/40629067.pdf, 11.

57. This switch was originally to have taken place on February 17, 2009, but the date was subsequently moved to June 2009. It may very well change again, however, as may the policies and procedures around the switch. Going digital is proving to be more complicated than many had initially imagined.

58. Quoted in Nate Anderson, "FCC Looks Set to Back 'White Spaces' as Chairman Signs On," *ars technica*, October 15, 2008, http://arstechnica.com/old/content/2008/10/fcc-looks-set-to-back-white-spaces-as-chairman-signs-on.ars.

59. Roy Mark, "Wireless Carriers: No Free Wireless Broadband for You," *eWeek*, July 24,2008, http://www.eweek.com/c/a/Mobile-and-Wireless/No-Free-Wireless-Broadband-for-You-Wireless-Carriers/.

60. "Bridging the Rural Digital Divide: FCC Starts Work on National Broadband Strategy," *Democracy Now!*, April 7, 2009, http://www.democracynow.org/2009/4/8/bridging_the_rural_digital_divide_fcc.

CHAPTER 3: GOING HYBRID: THE BIGGER PICTURE

1. Wes R. Habley and Randy McClanahan, *What Works in Student Retention—Two-Year Public Colleges* (ACT, 2004), 10.

2. Ibid.

3. "The NCTE Definition of 21st-Century Literacies," National Council of Teachers of English, February 5, 2008, http://www.ncte.org/about/over/positions/category/comp/129762.htm.

4. "The Horizon Report, 2008 Edition," The New Media Consortium and the Educause Learning Initiative, http://www.nmc.org/pdf/2008-Horizon-Report.pdf, 3.

5. Ibid., 7.

6. Ibid., 3.

7. Ibid., 5.

8. Ibid., 6.

9. Mandated course placement testing emerged as the most commonly cited response to retention issues; 87 percent of campuses reported using this kind of placement testing. Habley and McClanahan, *What Works in Student Retention*, 14.

10. Thomas Bailey and Vanessa Smith Morest, eds., *Defending the Community College Equity Agenda* (Baltimore: Johns Hopkins University Press, 2006). (Readers can find an overview and a summary of major findings from *Defending the Community College Equity Agenda* at http://ccrc.tc.columbia.edu/Publication.asp?UID=473.)

11. Ibid., 258.

12. Notably, Wes Habley, coordinator for ACT State Organizations, responded to my query regarding national retention data for online offerings in this way: "I do not know of a national study on this issue." Local studies are available, however, and they tend to tell similar stories.

13. Libby V. Morris and Catherine L. Finnegan, "Best Practices in Predicting and Encouraging Student Persistence and Achievement Online," *Journal of College Student Retention: Research, Theory and Practice* 10, no. 1 (2008–2009): 57.

14. Sarah Carr, "As Distance Education Comes of Age, the Challenge Is Keeping the Students," *Chronicle of Higher Education,* February 11, 2000, http://chronicle.com/free/v46/i23/23a00101.htm.

15. "Student Success and Retention in Online Courses," Bellevue Community College, November, 2006, http://www.sbctc.ctc.edu/docs/data/stdt_success_retention_in_online_courses_bcc.pdf, 3.

16. "Within Term Retention Report, 2007 Spring," Office of Research and Planning, College of DuPage, June 19, 2007.

17. "Grade Analysis—Fall 2006," Unpublished data, Liberal Arts, College of DuPage, August 27, 2008.

18. Wes Habley, personal correspondence with the author, August 28, 2008.

19. Jeffrey R. Young, "$4-a-Gallon Gas Drives More Students to Online Courses," *Chronicle of Higher Education,* July 18, 2008, http://chronicle.com/weekly/v54/i45/45a02001.htm.

20. "UIS Online and Blended Enrollment," Office of Technology-Enhanced Learning, University of Illinois at Springfield, http://otel.uis.edu/Portal/aboutOTEL/onlinegrowth.asp.

21. "Distance Education Enrollments at Illinois Colleges and Universities," Illinois Virtual Campus, Winter/Spring 2008, http://www.ivc.illinois.edu/pubs/enrollPDF/Spring08.pdf.

22. Elaine I. Allen and Jeff Seaman, "Making the Grade: Online Education in the United States, 2006" (Needham, MA: Sloan Consortium, 2006), 1.

23. Tara Brabazon, *Digital Hemlock: Internet Education and the Poisoning of Teaching* (Sydney: University of New South Wales Press, 2002). See also Tara Brabazon, *The University of Google* (Burlington, VT: Ashgate, 2007), and Marc Bousquet, *How the University Works: Higher Education and the Low-Wage Nation* (New York: New York University Press, 2008).

24. David Itzkhoff, "Obama Ads Appear in Video Game," Arts, Briefly, *New York Times,* October 14, 2008, http://www.nytimes.com/2008/10/15/arts/15arts-002.html?ref=arts.

25. "Obama Introduces Biden as Running Mate," CNN.com, August 23, 2008, http://www.cnn.com/2008/POLITICS/08/23/biden.democrat.vp.candidate/index.html.

26. "Barack Obama's Text Message to Supporters," Minnesota Public Radio, August 23, 2008, http://minnesota.publicradio.org/display/web/2008/08/23/obama_message/?refid=0.

27. "Welcome the Next Vice President," Barack Obama, http://my.barackobama.com/page/s/welcomejoe.

28. What is now Eddie Bauer Holding was once a subsidiary of Spiegel.

29. The Eddie Bauer homepage, including the "Creed," the "Guarantee," and an image of "Eddie Bauer's" signature, is at http://www.eddiebauer.com/.

30. A rather more interesting case of narrative collaboration actually occurs in the Wikipedia.org entry for "Eddie Bauer"; the content of the entry itself is not particularly remarkable, but the entry has been flagged, "This article or section is written like an advertisement" ("Eddie Bauer, Wikipedia"). This is followed by an invitation to "wikify" the section. In other words, it is a narrative waiting to happen.

31. "About REI," REI, http://www.rei.com/aboutrei/about_rei.html.

32. "Share Your REI Member Photos," REI, http://www.rei.com/member photos.

33. Henry Jenkins, *Convergence Culture Where Old and New Media Collide* (New York: New York University Press, 2006), 243.

34. "Cinemania," AMC, http://www.amctv.com/movienights/cinemania.

35. Jenkins, *Convergence Culture,* 18–19.

36. Ibid., 20.

37. Ibid., 28.

38. Survivor Fever, http://www.survivorfever.net/.

39. César G. Soriano, "Internet 'Survivor' Snoops Vie to Outscoop," Tech, *USAToday,* http://www.usatoday.com/tech/news/2001–01–26-survivor.htm.

40. Quoted in a post by Heliox, August 18, 2008, at Survivor Sucks, http://www.survivorsucks.com/.

41. Posted by IslandmanPT, August 26, 2008, at Survivor Sucks, http://www.survivorsucks.com/.

42. Denise Fields and Alan Fields, *Baby Bargains* (Boulder, CO: Windsor Peak Press, 2007).

43. "The Baby Boards: Baby Bargains and Baby 411," http://www.wind sorpeak.com/vbulletin/index.php.

44. An unfortunate aspect of the experiential knowledge that the Web can sometimes effectively provide has been the practice of companies paying bloggers and those on Facebook and Twitter to generate buzz about certain products or events. In other words, people are paid to express what looks, to other Web users, like personal opinion. Until now, at least, there has been no way for Web users to know what on the Web is genuine and what is paid endorsement. But the Federal Trade Commission has passed legislation that requires bloggers to disclose financial arrangements in cases where they have been paid to express an opinion. See "FTC: Bloggers Must Disclose Paid Endorsements," *All Things Considered,* National Public Radio, October 6, 2009, http://www-cdn.npr.org/templates/transcript/transcript.php?storyId=113548758.

45. The ESPN homepage is at http://espn.go.com/.

46. "SportsNation," ESPN, http://sportsnation.espn.go.com/.

47. A pull-down menu on the SportsNation Web page provides links to "Profiles," "Groups," "Conversations," "Chats," "Polls," "Message Boards," and "Widgets."

48. Jeffrey R. Young, "'Hybrid' Teaching Seeks to End the Divide between Traditional and Online Instruction," *Chronicle of Higher Education*, March 22, 2002, http://chronicle.com/free/v48/i28/28a03301.htm.

49. Michael Chabon, *Maps and Legends* (San Francisco: McSweeney's Books, 2008), 56.

50. One finds that Internet aliases tend toward either self-deprecation, as in "5BY5IDIOT," or to self-aggrandizement, "STUD24."

51. "Reason" is at http://www.fanfiction.net/s/4368603/1/Reason. The "Reason" "reviews" are at http://www.fanfiction.net/r/4368603/.

52. See http://www.fanfiction.net/book/Catcher_in_the_Rye/.

53. Ashley Highfield, "TV's Tipping Point: Why the Digital Revolution Is Only Just Beginning," BBC Press Office, October 6, 2003, http://www.bbc.co.uk/pressoffice/speeches/stories/highfield_rts.shtml.

54. David Folkenflik, "NYTimes.Com Exec Named New NPR CEO," National Public Radio, November 11, 2008, http://www.npr.org/templates/story/story.php?storyId=96875233.

55. Visit http://my.nytimes.com/ to register. As of December 15, 2008, the main nytimes.com Web site does not feature direct links to MyNyTimes, though the customizable MyTimes interface is still fully functional.

56. "Video Library Home Page," *New York Times*, http://video.on.nytimes.com/.

57. Folkenflik, "NYTimes.Com Exec Named New NPR CEO."

58. Ryan Singel follows technology and media trends for Wired.com and other news outlets. He is the author of numerous articles, including "New York Times Ponders Two Ways to Charge Online Readers." I contacted Singel regarding the *New York Times*' choice to go interactive and customizable through the my.nytimes feature and yet its subsequent move away from highlighting my.nytimes on the main NYTimes Web page. Singel suggested that, while "Personalization isn't going away," relatively few users take the time to fully customize a portal page like my.nytimes. Singel noted that "there's only a small percentage of people who take the time to set such things up."

59. See http://apps.pirates.go.com/pirates/v3/welcome.

60. "On Deck with the Developers," *Pirates of the Caribbean Online*, http://apps.pirates.go.com/pirates/v3/#/game_info/day_in_the_life.html.

61. Ibid.

62. "Grog Blog," *Pirates of the Caribbean Online*, http://blog.piratesonline.go.com/blog/pirates/.

63. "Pirates Online Launches Grog Blog," *Pirates of the Caribbean Online*, http://blog.piratesonline.go.com/blog/pirates/entry/what_do_you_think_of#comments.

64. James Paul Gee and Michael H. Levine, "Welcome to Our Virtual Worlds," *Educational Leadership*, March 2009, 49.

65. Mark Bauerlein, *The Dumbest Generation: How the Digital Age Stupefies Young Americans and Jeopardizes Our Future* (New York: Penguin, 2008).

66. The *World of Warcraft* homepage is at http://www.worldofwarcraft.com/index.xml; the *Ultima Online* homepage is at http://www.uoherald.com/.

67. A good example here is the Monster Hunter Freedom series for Sony's handheld PSP device. Some players have actually criticized Capcom game designers for making so much of the game content accessible only in multiplayer modes.

CHAPTER 4: HYBRIDS: A CULTURAL MOMENT AND ITS HISTORY

1. Steve Rosenbaum, "Is Obama a 'Hybrid'?" The Huffington Post, April 20, 2008, http://www.huffingtonpost.com/steve-rosenbaum/is-obama-a-hybrid_b_97661.html.

2. The video is on YouTube at http://www.youtube.com/watch?v=v9_7ElMpil8.

3. Quoted in Nishat Kurwa, "Urban Desi: A Genre on the Rise," *All Things Considered*, National Public Radio, October 15, 2008, http://www.npr.org/templates/story/story.php?storyId=95739927.

4. Ibid.

5. The comments are appended to Kurwa's report, http://www.npr.org/templates/story/story.php?storyId=95739927.

6. "The Birth of the Prius," CNN Money, February 24, 2006, http://money.cnn.com/magazines/fortune/fortune_archive/2006/03/06/8370702/.

7. Among many books that cover the development of education by correspondence, John Noffsinger, *Correspondence Schools* (New York: Macmillan, 1926), provides a useful and concise history.

8. Quoted in Noffsinger, *Correspondence Schools,* 5.

9. Ibid., 6.

10. Ibid., 8–13.

11. Ibid., 16.

12. The Distance Education and Training Council homepage can be found at http://www.detc.org/.

13. "Distance Education Survey—2007," Distance Education and Training Council, http://www.detc.org/downloads/2007DESurvey.pdf, 15.

14. Ads for "curriculum experts" or "subject matter experts" often show up on employment sites like http://www.monster.com/ and http://www.careerbuilder.com/. These job postings do not always last long, however.

15. "Evidence of Quality in Distance Education Programs Drawn from Interviews with the Accreditation Community," Office of Postsecondary Education, U.S. Department of Education, March, 2006, http://www.ysu.edu/accreditation/Resources/Accreditation-Evidence-of-Quality-in-DE-Programs.pdf, 5.

16. Ibid., 7.

17. Cary Nelson, foreword to *How the University Works: Higher Education and the Low-Wage Nation,* by Marc Bousquet (New York: New York University Press, 2008), xv.

18. David Noble, *Digital Diploma Mills* (New York: Monthly Review Press, 2001), 1.

19. The Education Management Corporation homepage is at http://www.edmc.com.

20. Governance and stock price information is at "Investor Relations," Education Management Corporation, http://phx.corporate-ir.net/phoenix.zhtml?c=87813&p=irol-irhome.

21. "Online High School Diploma," MUST High School, http://musthighschool.com/.

22. Illinois Board of Higher Education, http://www.ibhe.state.il.us/Links/institutions.asp.

23. Illinois Virtual Campus, http://www.ivc.illinois.edu/.

24. The Council for Higher Education Accreditation, http://www.chea.org/search/default.asp.

25. "Distance Education Survey—2007," Distance Education and Training Council, http://www.detc.org/downloads/2007DESurvey.pdf, 12.

26. "Diploma Mills," U.S. General Accounting Office, Testimony before the Committee on Governmental Affairs, U.S. Senate, May 11, 2004, http://www.gao.gov/new.items/d04771t.pdf.

27. Ibid., 2.

28. University of Northern Washington, http://www.unw.edu.

29. "UNW—Accreditation," University of Northern Washington, http://www.unw.edu/Accred.htm. The site goes on to say, however, that "the University of Northern Washington is accredited by the American Association of Private Post-Secondary Education, and our Business Administration and Information Systems programs have been critiqued, approved and accredited by the Institute of Financial Consultants and by the Institute of Computer and Professional Consultants, respectively." The American Association of Private Post-Secondary Education, the Institute of Financial Consultants, and the Institute of Computer and Professional Consultants are not listed in the CHEA directory for accrediting organizations.

30. Noble, *Digital Diploma Mills*, 6.

31. "College Learning for the New Global Century," National Leadership Council for Liberal Education and America's Promise, Association of American Colleges and Universities, 2007, http://www.aacu.org/leap/documents/GlobalCentury_final.pdf, 4.

32. Noble, *Digital Diploma Mills*, 7.

33. This particular job position was for an "enrollment counselor/account executive" at the University of Phoenix.

34. Noffsinger, *Correspondence Schools*, 24.

35. Ibid., 41–42.

36. Quoted in Goldie Blumenstyx, "Online Universities Are Gaining Acceptance, Pollster Says," *Chronicle of Higher Education,* August 12, 2008, http://chronicle.com/free/2008/08/4206n.htm.

37. Noffsinger, *Correspondence Schools*, 66.

38. "The Horizon Report, 2008 Edition," 5.

39. Yuri Kageyama, "Cellphone College Class Opens in Japan," *USAToday,* November 28, 2007, http://www.usatoday.com/tech/wireless/phones/2007–11–28-cellphone-college-japan_N.htm.

40. SoftBank holds a 71 percent stake in Cyber University.

CHAPTER 5: HYBRIDS IN ACTION

1. The Sloan Consortium defines a hybrid course as one that meets face-to-face for 30 percent or more of the course time.

2. This text happens to be from the College of DuPage class schedule that is provided online. Search the online listings for 10 colleges, though, and you will find 10 slightly different wordings. Or, in some cases, there may be *no* indication that a class listed in an online or print schedule is delivered in anything but the traditional mode.

3. The term "low-tech" here is value neutral; it simply helps to indicate that hybrids can use a wide variety of technologies.

4. *Community College Survey of Student Engagement: Committing to Student Engagement* (Bloomington, IN: Indiana Center for Postsecondary Research, 2008), 6.

5. Alma R. Clayton-Pedersen and Nancy O'Neill, "Curricula Designed to Meet 21st-Century Expectations," *Educating the Net Generation* (Educause, 2005), http://www.educause.edu/Resources/EducatingtheNetGeneration/CurriculaDesignedtoMeet21stCen/6065.

6. Ibid.

7. Virtual environments, like Second Life, provide interesting possibilities for realizing such "embodied" experiences online, however.

8. The cohort models means that students move through the program as a group. This obviously helps to develop a strong sense of community since students are together for an entire series of courses rather than just for one single class. The sense of connectedness that students develop through the cohort system can help to make the distance education portion of the program a much more engaging and communal experience. Cohort learning thus makes a nice complement to the hybrid program model.

9. Natasja Larson, "Faculty of Education Offers Blended Learning Masters Programs," unpublished memo, Faculty of Education, University of Alberta.

10. "Master of Educational Studies," University of Alberta, http://www.mes.ualberta.ca/general/frequentlyaskedquestions.html#traditional.

11. E-mail correspondence with the author, September 22, 2008.

12. Alfred P. Rovai and Hope M. Jordan, "Blended Learning and Sense of Community: A Comparative Analysis with Traditional and Fully Online Graduate Courses," *International Review of Research in Open and Distance Learning* 5, no. 2 (2004), http://www.irrodl.org/index.php/irrodl/article/view/192/274.

13. "Evidence of Quality in Distance Education Programs Drawn from Interviews with the Accreditation Community," U.S. Department of Education, Office of Postsecondary Education, March 2006, http://www.ysu.edu/accreditation/Resources/Accreditation-Evidence-of-Quality-in-DE-Programs.pdf, 2–3.

14. E-mail correspondence with the author, September 22, 2008.

15. The M.E.S. program technology checklist can be found at http://www.mes.ualberta.ca/pdfs/MESTechnologyCompliance1204.pdf. First on the checklist is: "I have regular access to a reasonably new computer." Third is: "I have

access to a high speed internet connection at home and/or at work." A signed copy of the checklist is to be included as part of students' application to the program. Efforts like this checklist should be applauded, and reliable access to a computer and the Internet is a priority. But, as we have seen in a number of cases already, while a high-speed Internet connection from home is recommended, it is not actually required.

16. Natasja Larson, "Faculty of Education Offers Blended Learning Masters Programs," unpublished memo, Faculty of Education, University of Alberta.

17. E-mail correspondence with the author, September 25, 2008.

18. Elluminate is a virtual meeting and distance learning platform that allows for a "moderator" to present material to a group of meeting participants. Features of Elluminate include a PowerPoint slide show presenter and remote computer desktop sharing, as well as standard virtual meeting software features like audio, video, and text-based chat.

19. E-mail correspondence with the author, September 25, 2008.

20. "Registration and Fees," Faculty of Graduate Studies and Research, University of Alberta, http://www.gradstudies.ualberta.ca/regfees/.

21. E-mail correspondence with the author, September 24, 2008.

22. LEEP originally stood for Library Education Experimental Program, though, now that the program is not "experimental," as it was when first offered in the mid-1990s, the acronym has become a word unto itself, rarely if ever receiving the full spell-out. Even the program Web pages now use the term with no explanation or indication of the acronym's origins.

23. "LEEP: Online Education," Graduate School of Library Information and Science, University of Illinois at Urbana-Champaign, http://www.lis.illinois.edu/programs/leep/.

24. See "LEEP: Library and Information Science," http://global.uillinois.edu/library-science-programs/master-of-science-in-library-and-information-science/. This page indicates that "Live Web-based instruction allows LEEP students to hear faculty, see slides and other graphics, and chat with the professor and each other. Students from as far away as Japan, Argentina, Mexico, France, Alaska, and Hawaii study together and develop a true learning community."

25. "LEEP: Online Education."

26. "Technology Requirements," http://www.lis.illinois.edu/programs/leep/#technology.

27. Paraphrased and directly quoted material comes from numerous e-mails that Emily and I traded in 2008 and 2009.

28. "LEEP: Online Education."

29. Marc Bousquet, *How the University Works: Higher Education and the Low-Wage Nation* (New York: New York University Press, 2008), 83.

30. "Costs," http://www.lis.illinois.edu/programs/leep/#costs.

31. E-mail correspondence with the author, November 10, 2008.

32. Ibid.

33. This and the following quotations come from student learning journals that have since been archived, which means they are no longer publicly accessible.

34. *Community College Survey of Student Engagement: Committing to Student Engagement*, 5.

35. E-mail correspondence with the author, November 4, 2008.

CHAPTER 6: TECHNOLOGY: TRENDING TO COMMUNITY AND COLLABORATION

1. This well-known study is often referred to as "nessie."

2. *National Survey of Student Engagement: Promoting Engagement for All Students* (Bloomington, IN: Indiana Center for Postsecondary Research, 2008), 35, 16.

3. Ibid., 16.

4. Don Tapscott and Anthony D. Williams, *Wikinomics: How Mass Collaboration Changes Everything* (New York: Portfolio, 2006), 1.

5. "MITOpenCourseWare," Massachusetts Institute of Technology, http://ocw.mit.edu/OcwWeb/web/about/about/.

6. "AboutUs," OpenCoursewareConsortium, http://www.ocwconsortium.org/about-us/about-us.html.

7. E-mail correspondence with the author, May 5, 2009.

8. Steve Lightstone, President of Corner Office Leads, is quoted in "Learn More about Google Sites," http://www.google.com/sites/help/intl/en/overview.html.

9. *National Survey of Student Engagement*, 6.

10. Ibid., 8.

11. *Community College Survey of Student Engagement*, 8.

12. I take this one step further. Having looked at everybody's homepage, I prepare a quiz that asks students in the class to identify which classmate corresponds to what hobby or interesting life detail. I might ask, "Who is interested in photography?" To answer the question, students must look through all of the class homepages.

13. To record and post video of myself I use a Logitech webcam, the software that came with the webcam, and a YouTube account. I am able to embed the HTML code from YouTube directly into my Blackboard course pages. There are innumerable variations, though, on how one might record video and put it into a course management system.

14. Aaron Barlow, *Blogging America: The New Public Sphere* (Westport, CT: Praeger), xi. See also Aaron Barlow, *The Rise of the Blogosphere* (Westport, CT: Praeger, 2007).

15. "'Blog' Picked as Word of the Year," BBC News: Technology, December 1, 2004, http://news.bbc.co.uk/2/hi/technology/4059291.stm.

16. Lev Grossman, "Time's Person of the Year: You," *Time*, December 13, 2006, http://www.time.com/time/magazine/article/0,9171,1569514,00.html.

17. Tapscott and Williams, *Wikinomics*, 1.

18. Barlow, *Blogging America*, 3.

19. Tapscott and Williams, *Wikinomics*, 10.

20. Barlow, *Blogging America*, 4. Italics are mine.

21. "Wikipedia," Wikipedia, http://en.wikipedia.org/wiki/Wikipedia.

22. "About," Wikipedia, http://en.wikipedia.org/wiki/About_Wikipedia. Italics are mine.

23. The episode of NBC's hit sitcom *30 Rock* entitled "Retreat to Move Forward" plays with the open editability of Wikipedia. One of the show's characters, Jenna Maroney, is studying for her role as Janis Joplin in an upcoming movie by conducting research on Wikipedia. As a practical joke, however, one of Jenna's co-workers, Frank, is entirely rewriting the Janis Joplin entry with wildly inaccurate information.

24. See http://wikitravel.org/en/Main_Page.

25. "Plunge Forward," Wikitravel, http://wikitravel.org/en/Wikitravel: Plunge_forward.

26. "How to Handle Unwanted Edits," Wikitravel, http://wikitravel.org/en/Wikitravel: How_to_handle_unwanted_edits. Italics are in the original.

27. The group member who does not contribute at all is not a problem. Unlike with traditional classroom group work, in which cases there may be no easy mechanism for ensuring that everybody contributes equally, an online wiki tracks and records the activity—or lack thereof—for all of its members.

28. James West and Margaret West, *Using Wikis for Online Collaboration: The Power of the Read-write Web* (San Francisco: Jossey-Bass, 2009), 127.

29. Ibid., 125.

30. Tapscott and Williams, *Wikinomics*, 41.

31. Delicious can be found at http://delicious.com. Sometimes the site is rendered as "del.icio.us," an earlier incarnation of the site name.

32. "Overview," Digg, http://digg.com/about/.

33. See http://delicious.com/help/learn and http://delicious.com/.

34. "How Digg Works," Digg, http://digg.com/how.

35. Meredith G. Farkas, *Social Software in Libraries* (Medford, NJ: Information Today, 2007), 130.

36. "Second Life Official Site," Second Life, http://secondlife.com/. Note that the homepage changes frequently, so new images, links, and text appear on a regular basis.

37. Script Me! (http://www.3greeneggs.com/autoscript/) generates LSL script based on user responses to basic questions like "What do you want your scripted object to do?" The resulting script can be cut and pasted into the Second Life script editor.

38. Bob Tedeschi, "Awaiting Real Sales from Virtual Shoppers," *New York Times*, June 11, 2007, http://www.nytimes.com/2007/06/11/business/11ecom.html.

39. Joseph Laszlo and Raz Schionning are quoted in Tedeschi, "Awaiting Real Sales from Virtual Shoppers,".

40. "Bradley University Island Opens on Second Life," Cullom-Davis Library, Bradley University, March 28, 2008, http://blogs.bradley.edu/library2/?p=62.

41. To visit places in Second Life, users first need to download and install the Second Life application from http://secondlife.com. The application includes a search function that allows users to find people and places.

42. Steve Taylor's Second Life avatar name is Stan Frangible.

43. Horowitz and Baldes chronicled their "road trip" at http://www. googlemapsroadtrip.com/. See also their interview with National Public Radio, "Taking the Great American Road Trip, Google-Style," *Morning Edition Sunday*, National Public Radio, April 16, 2009, http://www.npr.org/templates/ story/story.php?storyId=111921898. The comments attached to the interview debate whether or not the point was to replace "the real thing" with the "virtual."

44. The "Tintern Abbey" built in Second Life is the product of the amazing energy and talents of Denise Cote and Jenny Pompe, librarians at the College of DuPage.

45. Wordsworth used the phrase in Book 12 of his long poem entitled *The Prelude:* "There are in our existence spots of time, / That with distinct preeminence retain / A renovating virtue."

46. E-mail correspondence with the author, December 15, 2008.

47. See http://www.tuelearningcommunity.com/ and http://tuelearning community.com/vlci/.

48. See http://v.tstc.edu/.

49. "TSTC Takes One Small Step for Virtual Worlds, One Giant Leap for Virtual World Education," PRWeb, May 18, 2009, http://www.prweb.com/ releases/TSTC/virtual_education/prweb2419874.htm.

50. Diana G. Oblinger and James L. Oblinger, eds., *Educating the Net Generation* (n.p.: Educause, 2005), http://www.educause.edu/educatingthenetgen, 1.2.

51. Tapscott and Williams, *Wikinomics,* 125.

52. Gloria Hillard, "Finding a 'Second Life' Online," National Public Radio, February 5, 2005, http://www.npr.org/templates/story/story.php?storyId= 4488103.

53. Barlow, *Blogging America,* 7.

54. Ibid., 7, 8–9.

55. E-mail correspondence with the author, December 9, 2008.

56. Tom Funk, *Web 2.0 and Beyond* (Westport, CT: Praeger, 2008), 6.

57. Philip Rosedale, "Alter Egos," *Forbes,* May 7, 2007, http://www.forbes. com/forbes/2007/0507/076.html.

58. Quoted in Tapscott and Williams, *Wikinomics,* 124.

59. "How Meeting in Second Life Transformed IBM's Elite into Virtual World Believers," Second Life Grid, http://secondlifegrid.net/casestudies/ IBM.

60. Quoted in Tapscott and Williams, *Wikinomics,* 124.

61. "How Meeting in Second Life Transformed IBM's Elite into Virtual World Believers."

62. "Three Questions for Diane Berry, CEO of TPMA, on an Event in Second Life," Second Life Blogs, March 19, 2009, https://blogs.secondlife.com/ community/grid/blog/2009/03/19/three-questions-for-diane-berry-ceo-of-tpma-on-an-event-in-second-life.

63. See http://www.exitreality.com/.

64. Tapscott and Williams, *Wikinomics,* 38.

65. "Carl's Jr. and Hardee's Web Sites among First to Go 3D," Reuters, May 28, 2008, http://www.reuters.com/article/pressRelease/idUS141289+28-May-2008+PRN20080528.

66. Ibid.

67. E-mail correspondence with the author, April 20, 2009.

68. Funk, *Web 2.0 and Beyond*, 64.

CHAPTER 7: A RESISTANT EARLY ADOPTER ARGUES FOR HYBRIDITY

1. Noble, *Digital Diploma Mills*, xii.

2. Quoted in Oblinger, "Growing Up with Google," 12.

3. Bauerlein, *The Dumbest Generation*.

4. Gerald Graff, "Argument over Information," *MLA Newsletter*, Fall 2008, 3.

5. Ibid.

Index